Social exclusion and community development

Paul Henderson and Harry Salmon

First published in Great Britain in 2001 by
Community Development Foundation
60 Highbury Grove, London N5 2AG
Tel: 020 7226 5375
Fax: 020 7704 0313
Email: admin@cdf.org.uk

Cover design by The Bears Communications, Amsterdam
Typeset by Jacki Reason, London N8
Printed in Great Britain by Crowes Complete Print, Norwich

British Library Cataloguing-in-Publication Data
A record of this publication is available from the British Library

ISBN 1 901974 27 8

Community Development Foundation

The Community Development Foundation (CDF) is a non-departmental public body supported by the Active Community Unit of the Home Office. Its role is to pioneer, study and promote new forms of community development, in order to inform public policy, professional practice and community initiatives.

Set up in 1968, CDF strengthens communities by ensuring the effective participation of people in determining the conditions that affect their lives. A leading authority on community development and associated issues in the UK and mainland Europe, CDF works through:

- local action projects
- development of best practice
- research, evaluation and policy analysis
- consultancies and training programmes
- conferences and seminars
- information and publications.

CDF provides services to, and works in partnership with, public, private, community and voluntary organisations.

Contents

Foreword

There has been a tendency in Britain for community development work and national anti-poverty debates and initiatives to run on parallel tracks. The publication of this timely booklet marks the increasing, and welcome, convergence of the two. As its title suggests, much of the impetus for the convergence comes from the New Labour government's social exclusion strategy.

Of particular significance in this context is the work of the Social Exclusion Unit (SEU), which has resulted in the publication of the ambitious National Strategy Action Plan, *A New Commitment to Neighbourhood Renewal*. A key dimension to the plan is 'community empowerment': 'the government is committed to ensuring that communities' needs and priorities are to the fore in neighbourhood renewal and that residents of poor neighbourhoods have the tools to get involved in whatever way they want' (SEU, 2001, para 5.26). The plan emphasises that effective engagement with the community is one of the key indicators of the success of the new local strategic partnerships charged with implementation.

Although the term 'community development' is conspicuous by its absence in the National Strategy Action Plan, it is clear that the strategy will be heavily reliant on the expertise and experience built up by years of community development work. As the plan acknowledges, 'community involvement is a complex process' in which the sometimes conflicting views of communities of interest as well as communities of place need to be articulated.

Social Exclusion and Community Development underlines the contribution that community development can make to this process. The Action Plan opens up the potential for community development to move from the margin to the mainstream of government action to combat poverty and exclusion. This presents community development with an important challenge, as Henderson and Salmon make clear. At the same time, a community development perspective raises questions about aspects of the social exclusion strategy. Henderson and Salmon offer a number of salutary warnings:

- The philosophy and practice of community development does not sit easily with the often narrow conceptualisation of social exclusion adopted by the government. In particular, there is a potential tension between the heavy emphasis on paid work as the route out of social exclusion and the demands that the neighbourhood renewal strategy will make on residents. One of the complaints frequently made by community activists is that social security 'availability for work' rules deter unemployed residents from community involvement. In response, the government has announced a trial relaxation of the rules. Yet this does not address the underlying issue of the overriding obligation to undertake paid work, regardless of any contribution made through unpaid work in the community. I have suggested elsewhere (Lister, 2001) that the government should consider pilot schemes under which benefit recipients involved in approved community or voluntary work could be exempted from the normal job-seeking requirements if they so wish. Such an approach has been tried successfully in the Netherlands where it has proved to be a useful way of both acknowledging the value of such work and of promoting social inclusion. The pilots could be introduced in some of the areas covered by the action plan.

- A central principle of community development is that community involvement cannot be imposed or made obligatory. Henderson and Salmon suggest that the action plan may be placing unrealistic expectations and undue responsibilities on those living in deprived neighbourhoods. One of the plan's strengths – that it involves a coherent national strategy, rather than simply a number of separate fragmented projects – also represents a potential source of friction with the welcome emphasis on community involvement. As the authors ask, what happens if the priorities of the national strategy and those of local residents do not coincide?

- A danger with any area-based strategy is that it may reinforce the negative labelling of the individuals and communities who are targeted for help. Increasingly the politics of poverty is involving resistance not just to economic forms of injustice but also to what has been termed 'cultural injustice'. This involves challenging the stigmatising ways in which marginalised groups are often represented in the wider society. It raises demands for respect and recognition of marginalised people as equal citizens whose voices have a right to be heard. The lack of respect for people living in poverty was 'one of the clearest and most heartfelt messages' received by the independent Commission on Poverty, Participation and Power (2000, p3). While the Commission found many people living in poverty keen to be involved, as Henderson and Salmon warn, years of being ignored or sidelined, or experience of phoney participation, have also left many angry and disillusioned. Again, it will require painstaking and long-term

community development work, together with a commitment to
genuine involvement, to win over the sceptical and disillusioned.

- Finally, though, community development is no panacea, as Henderson
  and Salmon are at pains to emphasise. Community development has
  an important role to play in the recognition and promotion of the
  actions of people and communities suffering poverty and social
  exclusion. This helps to challenge images of helpless and passive
  victimhood, which are increasingly at odds with both the politics and
  theorising of poverty ad exclusion. However, both the politics and the
  theory emphasise the continued power of structural inequalities,
  which constrain that agency and which limit what can be achieved at
  neighbourhood level alone. As the authors argue, a genuinely 'joined
  up' strategy requires linking geographically based initiatives that
  promote community empowerment with macro-policies that address
  the wider structural causes of poverty and social exclusion.

Ruth Lister
Professor of Social Policy, Loughborough University and CDF Trustee

Acknowledgements

This publication arose out of the authors' twin commitments to the principles of community development and to the reduction of inequality between poor and rich neighbourhoods. We are grateful to the Community Development Foundation for making the publication possible and to Alison West (Chief Executive), Gabriel Chanan (Director, Dissemination), Stuart Hashagen (Manager, Scotland) and Ruth Lister (Trustee) for their comments on the draft text. Needless to say, responsibility for the views expressed remains with the authors.

We were delighted that Professor Ruth Lister agreed to write the foreword because much of her own work brings together the anti-poverty and community action/user involvement perspectives. We thank her for her contribution.

We acknowledge our debt to leaders of neighbourhood groups in deprived areas who willingly expressed their views; to officers in Coventry's Development Directorate for providing statistical information; and to the Area Co-ordinator covering Hillfields for his willingness to talk about the area and for reading paragraphs referring to it. Civil servants in the Social Exclusion Unit and the then Department of the Environment, Transport and the Regions helped by responding to enquiries quickly and efficiently.

Lawrence and Wishart have kindly allowed one of the authors to draw upon copyright material which first appeared in an article in Renewal. We also acknowledge use made of material from The Poverty Alliance and Cutteslowe Community Network.

1   Setting the scene

This publication explores the relationship between social exclusion and community development in relation to the renewal of neighbourhoods and examines the distinctive contribution that community development can make to this undertaking. It will be useful to a wide range of people including policymakers, managers, members of local authorities, partnership boards, voluntary agencies and those working on the ground.

It is important to state the publication's aim at the outset because, while we include substantive material on both social exclusion and community development, the booklet does not attempt to deal with each of them comprehensively. It is an assessment of the connections between social exclusion and community development, not an explanation of each of them, and the assessment concentrates mainly on the community development dimension of the connection. We set out to examine a sequence of challenges that we believe face community development:

- Analysis of community development principles as these relate to social exclusion.

- Discussion of the record of community development when using social exclusion criteria.

- Assessment of the potential of community development to deliver on objectives aimed at combating social exclusion.

Thus, if we assume that the focus of community development work has always been on exclusion, our interest lies in seeing how this claim stands up to examination and in discussing whether the government's emphasis on neighbourhood renewal presents new opportunities for community development.

Social exclusion

In opposition in the 1990s, Labour had begun to examine how it would address the growing social problems and increasing inequalities resulting from a long period of right-of-centre government. After the election defeat in 1992, John Smith set up a Commission on Social Justice. Its final report, *Social Justice: Strategies for National Renewal* (1994), was generally welcomed as an attempt to outline a programme for a future Labour government. However, those who had reservations about it noted the way in which the relationship between social justice and the market was being redefined. The report divided reformers into three categories – Deregulators, Investors and Levellers:

> *Unlike the Deregulators, who would use insecurity as the spur to change, the Investors insist on security as the foundation of change; but unlike the Levellers, the Investors achieve security by redistributing opportunities rather than just redistributing income.* (p95)

Having emphasised the relationship between the economy and social cohesion, it is not surprising that the report opted for the Investor approach. Reference to the Commission's work is rarely made, and though its emphasis on opportunity is reflected in the work of the Social Exclusion Unit (SEU), this probably owes more to the policies and speeches of ministers during the first months of Labour government than to the report.

The SEU is located in the Cabinet Office and reports directly to the Prime Minister, who formally launched it in December 1997. He asked it to report on 'how to develop integrated and sustainable approaches to the problems of the worst housing estates, including crime, drugs, unemployment, community breakdown and bad schools'. Since then it has published three reports – *Bringing Britain Together: A National Strategy for Neighbourhood Renewal* (1998), *National Strategy for Neighbourhood Renewal: A Framework for Consultation* (2000a) and *A New Commitment to Neighbourhood Renewal* (2001). The most recent report proposed setting up a Neighbourhood Renewal Unit (NRU) in the then Department of the Environment, Transport and the Regions (DETR), and this has now been established. A Cabinet-level committee is chaired by the Deputy Prime Minister. It is possible, of course, that the government elected in June 2001 may change these arrangements.

Renewing neighbourhoods

From its inception neighbourhood renewal has been the overarching theme of the SEU's work. Identifying the most deprived neighbourhoods was not easy. *Bringing Britain Together* draws upon different sets of criteria which produce a wide range of figures. It eventually identified the 1200 to 1600 most deprived neighbourhoods and estates. Revised indices of deprivation drawn up in 2000 by the DETR (2000a) helped the SEU to narrow its focus.

The National Strategy for Neighbourhood Renewal attributes neighbourhood decay mainly to economic factors and consequent unemployment and describes the aim of the strategy as:

> *...to arrest the wholesale decline of deprived neighbourhoods, to reverse it, and prevent it from recurring.*
> *Success should be measured against a simple goal – to narrow the gap between deprived areas and the rest of the country by dramatically improving*

outcomes – with more jobs, better educational attainment, less crime and better health – in the most deprived areas. (p9)

The 2001 SEU report says that 10 per cent of the neighbourhoods identified are 'seriously deprived': 82 per cent of these are concentrated within the boundaries of 88 local authorities. This covers 693 of the seriously deprived wards, on which the government intends to concentrate, and whose geographical distribution is set out in the report. A Neighbourhood Renewal Fund (NRF) will provide substantial sums to support regeneration in these deprived areas.

No one concerned with the conditions in which large numbers of our fellow citizens have to live can quarrel with the aims expressed in the executive summary and reflected throughout the report.

Co-ordinated responses

A recurring phrase is 'joined-up solutions to joined-up problems'. The need for this has long been recognised by those working on the ground, and it will be a great advance if 'joined-up solutions' are delivered. Given the complexity of the problems, the structures of government at every level and the need to involve local people as well as other agencies, the difficulties should not be underestimated.

Plowden points out that though the language has changed, the idea has been around since the 1970s. In the 1980s he was an author of a research report into why an attempt to formulate a 'joint approach to social policy' in the 1970s failed. For the new initiative to succeed, Plowden says it is first essential that 'Whitehall should get its various acts together', and that it must then give local authorities the freedom to act and make the necessary local connections (*The Guardian*, 8 March 2000).

Local authorities have been given a prominent role in the delivery of 'joined-up' solutions and government has directed them to use mainstream services to tackle social exclusion. 'Mainstreaming' is not about using budgets designated for short-term initiatives, but about 'how ... budgets can be bent to address specific needs of particular groups or address specific issues' (Woods, 2000, p7). It is also about promoting partnerships.

SEU's first steps

In response to SEU's 1998 report, 18 theme-based Policy Action Teams (PATs) were set up consisting of Whitehall officials, experts on the topics and people working in deprived areas. Each PAT had a 'ministerial champion'. All produced reports and, in addition, four reports 'on the analysis of particular aspects of social exclusion' were published. These deal with:

- Truancy and social exclusion – 1998.
- Rough sleeping – 1998.
- Teenage pregnancy – 1999.
- Bridging the gap: new opportunities for 16-18 year olds not in education, employment or training – 1999.

Participation and self-help

It is commendable that the SEU is reversing the old 'top-down' approach. In recent years governments have increasingly made evidence of local people's involvement a condition of funding for special projects, but participation has never before been so clearly enunciated as it is in the strategy for neighbourhood renewal. Though several reports refer to this, it is PAT 9's report on community self-help that deals most fully with the involvement of local people, and it does this thoroughly (Home Office, 1999). It also makes clear recommendations, but we have reservations about its underlying philosophy and about some of its recommendations, which we will deal with later.

Participation and the involvement of local people is central to our other major theme – the contribution community development can make to dealing with social exclusion and promoting social inclusion. While self-help schemes sometimes emerge from the community development process the latter does not set out to promote such schemes.

The SEU's reports rarely refer to community development and it is unclear, therefore, whether the unit assumes that local people will become involved spontaneously or whether it believes that good local publicity and gentle urging by local government officers and voluntary agency representatives will be enough. If it is the latter, then experience is likely to show that this rarely happens, particularly if the intention is to engage the most socially excluded. Usually the intervention of an experienced community development worker is required to encourage involvement by those lacking the confidence and skills to work collectively.

Why is it that a burden of expectation and responsibility is placed upon the most socially and economically deprived when it is not placed on those of us who are socially and economically secure and living in areas not in need of renewal? Given that this publication is primarily about social exclusion and the relevance of community development, it is important that this question should be explored at the beginning, as it arises out of deeper questions about how the excluded are seen and valued.

On the moral question, community development's position is clear. Its principles can, in theory, be applied to any kind of milieu. For example, some churches have applied these principles to their own institutional life since the late 1960s. However, community development in practice concentrates on working in the most deprived areas on the grounds that people living in prosperous areas are likely to have the capacity to work on issues and projects of their own choosing. In addition, community development has had to prioritise its work carefully because of inadequate and uncertain resourcing.

Those engaged in community development do not begin with an assumption that the excluded should do more to help themselves – as PAT 9's report implies – but that they should be afforded the support to develop any response which they think appropriate and to develop the kind of skills (administrative, organisational, financial) which are abundant in suburbia. The only qualification would be a refusal to support groups if they decided to pursue discriminatory objectives.

Theory and ideology

There has been a tendency in the West to develop theories of poverty and deprivation which have laid most of the blame on the 'victims'. In the late 1960s Oscar Lewis popularised his culture of poverty theory, though Byrne (1999) believes this was intended to show how the poor positively and collectively developed ways of adapting to their conditions. Keith Joseph, Thatcher's intellectual mentor, gave the theory a moralistic and pathological twist in his notion of a cycle of deprivation. Today we have Charles Murray (1990, 1994) promoting his ideas about an 'underclass' – a term which occasionally slips into the vocabulary of some politicians and commentators.

There is, Byrne believes, a serious flaw in these approaches, in that while spelling out theories that people have become trapped in a self-perpetuating syndrome of anti-social practices, they are expected to break out and display moral responsibility. Amitai Etzioni's early brand of communitarianism, with its neglect of the responsibilities of the rich and powerful and its stress on 'communities' resolving their own problems, betrays the same tendency. We make a similar point as Byrne when we refer to Etzioni's failure 'to address the social responsibilities of governments, public agencies and private corporations' (Henderson and Salmon, 1998, p27).

When government ministers talk about social exclusion and ways in which it can be eradicated, they send out confusing signals. At times they seem to adopt an almost social pathology approach – sometimes it is about tough and more punitive measures to force people to fit into mainstream society, and on other occasions they take an exhortatory line, encouraging people to participate in initiatives aimed at tackling social exclusion. But there are also occasions when they acknowledge that the material conditions in which many live contribute to their experience of exclusion.

This issue has been explored here because, while there is much that is commendable in the reports produced by the SEU, occasionally there are phrases which suggest that the excluded are still seen as part of the problem and that too much responsibility for delivering solutions is being placed on them. Often people in deprived neighbourhoods wish to become engaged in self-help, but in community development it is left to choice and not to pressure.

Community development principles

Community development workers have been active in deprived areas since the late 1960s. Their work has consistently been based upon a number of principles. These can be summarised as:

- Residents have a right to be consulted about decisions that affect their area and this should be done in imaginative and appropriate ways.
- Involvement in community groups should be entirely a matter of choice and not of coercion.
- Local people should be supported in achieving their own goals provided these are not discriminatory.
- The pace of development should be determined by the participants and not by external agencies' needs.
- The worker should never usurp the role of a local leader.

A worker needs to be free to work with the 'agenda' of local people rather than with one imposed by an external agency. This is an issue which has frequently given rise to difficulties between workers and their employers.

Being realistic

The SEU reports emphasise the importance of 'capacity building' and the development of local leadership. There is also a recognition that these cannot be achieved quickly and, given that in the past community development has suffered from short-term funding, this is a welcome sign. It is also encouraging that the Prime Minister is talking of a ten to twenty year programme of neighbourhood renewal. However, some of the material conveys an exaggerated view of what can be achieved through the involvement of local people. There is a danger of indulging in the over-optimism of the 1970s when there were high expectations of the government's 12 community development projects (CDPs) and of the introduction of community workers into many neighbourhoods. The achievements of that period were useful but modest and most of the groups and organisations which emerged had a short life span – frequently two to seven years. The mistakes were the failure to recognise the deep structural problems which could not be resolved entirely through locally based initiatives and the difficulties of sustaining on-going community involvement.

A look at what has happened in deprived areas targeted in the 1970s provides a salutary lesson. Hillfields in Coventry is such an example. From late 1969 to the early 1980s there were sustained efforts to involve people in community activities. From 1970 to 1975 one of the 12 CDPs was based in the area. It was staffed by a committed team and, when the project ceased, most of the workers stayed in the area and established an independent agency. There was also community work input from city-wide voluntary agencies. Throughout this period there was a consistent policy of community 'capacity building' – though that phrase was not in vogue at the time. During the mid-1970s the local authority opened its first purpose-built community comprehensive school in Hillfields and the initial community team was deeply committed to working beyond the walls of the school.

The story of that period can be told either as a success or failure, according to which aspects the teller selects. Briefly recording both sides of the story will help to set the government's neighbourhood renewal initiative in an historical context.

Success and failure

Work started in 1969 from an exceptionally low baseline. Apart from faith-based institutions, the only neighbourhood organisations were a 'community' association which consisted of five professionals who worked in Hillfields, one pre-school playgroup organised by a person from outside the area, a struggling tenants' group based on the 11 tower blocks and a group of young communists who daubed slogans, put out leaflets and soon disappeared.

In the course of six years, more than 20 community groups came into existence and other short-life action groups formed around particular issues – some were successful, others collapsed. Local leaders emerged, a few people acquired new skills and grew in confidence. For three years a monthly newspaper – *Hillfields Voice* – was produced and distributed free through 5000 letter boxes.

The community association became a strong co-ordinating body consisting of 22 locally controlled groups and handling a large budget. It was jealous of its identity as an organisation run by the people of Hillfields and the supporting community worker was the only professional allowed to attend its meetings. Councillors and officers could only attend by invitation. It employed a local person to develop work amongst older people and two adventure playground leaders, and local people were trained to run an information and opinion centre. Two General Improvement Areas were designated, as a result of effective campaigns aided by a CDP planner. A strong action group fought a successful campaign to modify a redevelopment plan for another part of the area. The community association led a sustained campaign over four years to get a community centre which they would control, and they eventually succeeded. Though the community association was unhappy about the setting up of a community school – especially as it resulted in the demolition of several streets – after its own major goal was achieved an accommodation with the school developed and a community representative joined the governing body.

During the same period the local authority, with Urban Aid funding, established an imaginative nursery and play centre at the heart of the 11 tower block complex. A few cosmetic environmental improvements were carried out. An imaginative community education programme was initiated by CDP and adopted by the local education authority.

But in terms of the kind of objectives referred to in reports from the SEU, the work largely failed. Today agencies are engaged in a re-run of earlier initiatives. The *New Hillfields Times* – 'a newsletter from the Company founded to regenerate your area' – is a politically milder version of the original *Hillfields Voice*. While environmental and housing improvements have continued, banks have disappeared, as have many shops, though a small new shopping complex has now been built. The tower blocks remain unpopular even though a system of concierges is being established – the kind of initiative which tenants were requesting in the early 1970s. New forms of crime have emerged to replace the prostitution that was previously rampant. In December 1999 the crime figures were far higher than for any other ward in the city, and unemployment figures are still failing to match the city's improved employment situation. In June 2000 male unemployment was 15.3 per cent as against a city average of 6.7 per cent; in 1971 it stood at 7.8 per cent, against a city average of 4.2 per cent. Despite 'on the ground' projects to help unemployed people get jobs, the figures are now worse, compared with the city average, than they were in 1971. After a lapse of nearly 20 years, the process of renewal has started again. It would seem that the title of the first part of Coventry CDP's last report to the Home Office and the City Council, in association with the Institute of Local Government Studies, was prescient: *Coventry and Hillfields: Prosperity and the Persistence of Inequality* (1975).

This cameo of a deprived neighbourhood is in no way exceptional. Some readers will be able to name similar examples. Liverpool is an example of a city where community workers abounded in the 1970s and there were vigorous local groups. The city has witnessed almost the whole range of government schemes aimed at regeneration, and yet unemployment remains high and the inequalities between different parts of Merseyside remain stark. The question is whether the present programme will achieve its stated aims or whether, in 30 years' time, governments will still be baffled by the continuing wide disparities between neighbourhoods.

The Hillfields example is included in the introduction so that the more theoretical chapters can be considered against the backcloth of a real situation. It does not detract from the value of community development, but it does emphasise the need for two things. The first is that local intervention of any kind is more productive if located within a long-term government strategy to reduce inequality. This would have to include the provision of work through the public sector to compensate for the failure of the economy to generate enough jobs in the travel to work area. Secondly, community development and other forms of local intervention may need to be continued over long periods if strong and representative local organisations are to be sustained.

Key words

There are three terms that figure prominently in the SEU's literature which have already been used several times. Each is capable of being given a different emphasis. As far as possible, we are seeking to be consistent, and it might help if we clarify our use of the terms at this point.

Exclusion

Increasingly 'inclusion' is being used instead of the more negative sounding 'exclusion'.

Observant readers will note that we move between the two words – the latter when we are writing in government mode and the former when we are reflecting our personal preference. We recognise that this also runs into semantic difficulties. As Gray (2000) points out, inclusion may or may not contribute to equality.

Deprivation

In the early 1970s there were heated debates about ways of describing the plight of inner city areas. Each term used conveyed its own ideological baggage. Deprivation was out, largely because of its association with the 'cycle of deprivation' theory. However, the debate has moved on. The SEU usually uses 'deprivation' and we do the same. Our concern is with the way in which neighbourhoods are 'deprived' primarily by factors beyond the control of the people themselves.

Community

'Community' must be one of the most abused words in the English language. It is repeatedly used without necessarily differentiating between a body of people bound by some of the recognised characteristics of 'community' and a collection of people living in a neighbourhood. Those who have written the SEU's reports have shown some understanding in referring to deprived neighbourhoods rather than deprived communities. However, although in the self-help report PAT 9 (Home Office, 1999) there are indications that the authors are aware of some of the characteristics of a community – for example, stability, family links, friendship networks – they frequently apply the word 'community' without knowing whether it is a community or simply a neighbourhood. Later, we will make reference to the way in which an apparent failure to understand the complex dynamics of neighbourhoods led to some weaknesses in PAT 9's presentation. For our part, we will seek to be economical and disciplined in our use of 'community'.

Outline of contents

The sequencing of the publication is straightforward, moving from an analysis of social exclusion to a discussion of how community development has engaged with it and the potential for the future.

In chapter 2 we explore the semantic and ideological arguments surrounding social exclusion and summarise the factors which, together or separately, constitute the reality of social exclusion. Chapter 3 concentrates on the relationship between community development and social exclusion, with particular reference to community development's experience of working with the most marginalised and deprived members of society. The purpose is to identify key lessons which policymakers responsible for implementing social inclusion strategies need to learn, and to highlight the opportunities presented to community development by the SEU's agenda.

In chapter 4 we look more closely at the practice of community development in relation to social inclusion: what can be learnt from this experience; what guidelines it offers for the future. In the conclusion, we summarise the arguments and draw out the lessons, both for those responsible for the implementation of the National Strategy for Neighbourhood Renewal and for agencies and workers engaged in community development with those deemed to be socially excluded.

2 The meaning of social exclusion

The purpose of this chapter is to prepare the ground for a realistic assessment of the part that community development can play in combating social exclusion and promoting the values of a more cohesive society.

There is now a considerable literature on social exclusion. It is both a controversial and complex concept. Following a brief introduction on how the term entered our vocabulary, the chapter opens up some of the issues surrounding it, and then describes its different facets and identifies its consequences. References are made to broader government policies where these have a bearing on the subject.

Background

The term 'social exclusion' emerged out of the European Anti-Poverty Programmes during the 1980s and early 1990s, though as Room (1993) points out, as late as 1984 the Council of European Communities was defining the objectives of the Anti-Poverty Programme as combating poverty and attacking its causes. But in the late 1980s France objected to the word 'poverty' and expressed a preference for 'social exclusion'. After the second round of projects under the Programme (1986-89), the term was widely adopted, the European Observatory on Policies to Combat Social Exclusion was set up, and social exclusion became a major theme of the third European Anti-Poverty Programme (1989-94). When Britain and Germany blocked the Commission's proposal for a fourth programme, the Observatory was closed down, but by then social exclusion was firmly established in the vocabulary of policymakers, politicians, academics and commentators. A fuller account of this transition from the vocabulary of poverty to that of social exclusion is provided by Room (op. cit.).

The French preference for the term social exclusion originated within its social policy, which places a stress on moral integration and social order. This emphasises the need for people to have strong ties with their families and culture. Later it became associated with more structural factors concerned with the marginalisation of particular groups and the plight of some outer suburbs in cities such as Paris and Marseilles.

Social exclusion and ideology

In this country, where the term social exclusion has a very short history, people tend to inject into it their own values, ideas and assumptions. Levitas (1998) identifies 'three discourses of social exclusion'. The first is redistributionist and is mainly concerned with poverty, the second is based upon the notion of an 'underclass' with its own pathology, and the third is social integrationist, concentrates on paid work, and is based upon a mixture of opportunities and coercion. In chapter 1 we made brief reference to theories which underpin the second discourse. Levitas illustrates the way in which politicians' definitions of social exclusion move uneasily between any two or even all three interpretations. The second and third discourses are more often reflected than the first one, though Blair's undertaking to 'eradicate child poverty in 20 years' requires redistribution of resources if it is to be achieved. According to an audit published by the Child Poverty Action Group (Fimister, 2001), good progress is being made. There is the prospect that the government could halve child poverty in five years.

Language is important. The terms used reflect deep changes in attitude and ideology. References to power, inequality, class and poverty are now few, but references to social exclusion, social cohesion, the underclass and opportunity are many. Yet, as Ruth Levitas points out, the use of words such as exclusion and inclusion hides the extent of inequalities and encourages the view that all that is required is more opportunity for everyone and marginal shifts of money to those who are poorest. The 'very rich are discursively absorbed into the included majority ...' (op. cit., p7).

In Scotland there has been criticism of the concept of social exclusion. Damien Killeen, Director of the Poverty Alliance, points out that when the Scottish Office undertook a national consultation on the nature of social exclusion and ways of tackling it, a majority of the 200 respondents regarded the main priority as being the redistribution of wealth through the tax and benefit systems (Killeen, 1999). The term 'social exclusion' was also seen as being divisive and discriminatory and there was a clear preference for a policy based on the principle of 'social inclusion'. Geddes (2000), in reviewing the Scottish approach to the issue, highlights the prominence given to the notion of 'inclusion' by local authorities.

Scotland has also recognised the importance of creating an 'intermediate labour market' in those parts of the country where it has not been possible to attract enough private investment to create jobs at the rate required to absorb all those who are unemployed. Paid work is being provided in socially useful activities. The purpose is to create jobs for those who have not been able to obtain work in the private sector. People are paid at the rate for the job on short-term contracts. This is seen as another way of promoting a sense of inclusion.

Fairclough (2000) points out that language has always been important in politics and in government for conveying ideological messages. Having this in mind, he analyses how it is used in Labour texts and particularly by the Prime Minister. He detects significant nuances in the way in which some key themes are referred to. In the period covered by his research, he found 44 references to 'exclusion', but only nine uses of the verb 'exclude'. He deduces from this that the emphasis is on outcome rather than process, dealing with the consequences of exclusion rather than with preventing it.

Although social exclusion can be interpreted in a way that evades broad structural consideration, this should not blind us to its positive features. In the first place, it does provide the possibility of raising questions about who is doing the excluding and by what process. Secondly, as we describe below, social exclusion has many facets, and as long as people do not lose sight of the 'big picture', it provides the possibility of responses being focused on particular aspects by people with relevant knowledge and skills. For example, community development can work with people in a way that enhances their self-worth and enables them to develop the skills to achieve self-determined objectives, but by itself it cannot bring significantly greater prosperity to an area.

Thirdly, one of the positive features of social exclusion is that it is a dynamic, not a static concept. It allows for movement and recognises the interaction between various elements. For example, acquiring a vocational skill or even getting a job does not necessarily bring someone out of a state of exclusion. Both Atkinson (1998) and Lister (2000) point out that a job does not necessarily end the state of exclusion. It depends upon remuneration and the job's degree of permanence. It may, however, provide a stepping stone to genuine inclusion.

Dynamism and social exclusion

Social exclusion is multi-dimensional, involving many different elements and ranging from the individual to the global. Ruth Lister says it 'encourages a focus on process rather than simply outcomes. In doing so it draws attention to both agency and structure. It 'implies that someone or something is excluding someone else and encourages us to examine the mechanisms involved' (ibid., p38).

Byrne (1999) analyses the way in which dynamic processes of change can also affect social exclusion. Even in the most deprived neighbourhoods long-term studies show how individuals and families have trajectories which can quite quickly change their situations. For example, a single mother on benefit may establish a stable relationship with a man in employment. This may enable the woman to get a part-time job, and this in turn could make it possible for them to move into a 'better bit' of the area. In Hillfields, the personal trajectories of a few people changed because of their involvement in neighbourhood activities. Over three or four years they developed skills, confidence and personal contacts with professional workers which opened up new possibilities. One by one they moved into forms of training, enabling them to gain qualifications which then allowed them to take up employment in community work, welfare rights or social work. In the process they all became geographically mobile and moved out of the area.

Ministers would see this last illustration as an example of the kind of outcome that the neighbourhood renewal policies are intended to achieve: improving people's 'employability' – in this instance through community involvement and training – makes it possible for them to climb out of social exclusion. But many people in areas selected for neighbourhood renewal do not acquire such opportunities. Most of the inhabitants of Hillfields remained trapped, though some did have improved houses or new homes, and when people managed to move out – often from the disliked tower blocks – there were always those whose personal or family trajectory was such that they were prepared to move in. Thus the spatial dimension of social exclusion is perpetuated – and often deepened.

Those who achieve upward spatial mobility benefit in many ways – it is more than a sign of improved economic status. It often means easier access to financial services, a better environment and housing, less exposure to crime and better schools. Indeed, those who are already living in such areas sometimes use their greater financial security to make a further move into the catchment area of a school noted for its academic results. The government's intense interest in renewing neighbourhoods is a clear recognition of this spatial dimension.

Unfortunately, however, dynamism of a different kind can impact unfavourably upon attempts to combat exclusion. Byrne (ibid.) argues that the global economy results in dynamic processes which generate spatial problems at different geographical levels, from the national to the local. He believes that they are an inevitable consequence of post-industrial capitalism within a global financial system. From a very different ideological perspective, John Gray makes a similar point. He believes that: 'Global laissez-faire is no less inimical to the project of an inclusive society' as it is to the egalitarian values of classical social democracy (Gray, 2000, p33). The consequences are that global flows of capital which are constantly in search of higher returns can quickly affect economic stability. This means, he maintains, that governments may have to consider placing political constraints on financial globalisation.

Therborn (1985) believes that 'advanced capitalism' results in a social structure divided into the emmiserated poor (Byrne, op.cit., p55), a reasonably comfortable but less secure middle band, and an increasingly rich, powerful elite who are drifting away from the rest of society in terms of both wealth and lifestyle and who believe their privileged status is justified. This latter group is self-excluded from the rest of society.

'Measuring' social exclusion

While social exclusion is now the preferred term, its analysis depends upon using familiar categories. The SEU's PAT 18 on better information drew upon a paper reviewing indices for 'measuring deprivation' – a long established term. This exercise underlined how many different components have to be taken into account. There is no single set of indices covering all the factors associated with social exclusion. Eight specific sets are summarised and reference is made to three geo-demographic systems. Bodies such as health authorities/departments, the Department of Transport, Local Government and the Regions (DTLR) and local authorities depend upon different criteria. However, the then Department of the Environment, Transport and the Regions (DETR) introduced new indices of deprivation that also take into account rural poverty (DETR, 2000a).

PAT 18's first report recommended that by April 2001 neighbourhood statistics containing ward level data should be available electronically at no charge, and that following the publication of the 2001 census during 2002-3 the government should expand these to provide an on-going source of data. Eventually – if fully implemented – these recommendations should prove helpful to community leaders and workers on the ground as well as to policymakers, but an undue emphasis on better information can suggest that the required response is a series of minor operations on the excluded rather than major surgery on the whole system.

There are also technical problems with accurate information gathering. For instance, ward boundaries do not necessarily reflect neighbourhood boundaries, and are neighbourhoods based upon a government or agency definition or upon the perceptions of local people? How do we measure social and psychological factors such as how people 'feel' about their localities and how their environment affects their attitudes towards others? The movement of people in some areas is almost impossible to monitor.

Web of social exclusion

Whilst there are many factors involved in individual, family and neighbourhood experiences of social exclusion, there are two general observations to make. The first is that social exclusion will not be prevented without changes in the wider social and economic system. The second is that the lack of adequate income is nearly always a factor in exclusion from mainstream society. That is why Levitas is right to stress the importance of the 'redistributionist discourse', whereas in government circles and in Europe the 'social integrationist' approach has been dominant.

As long as the analogy is not pressed too far, social exclusion can be visualised as a web consisting of a number of linked elements in which people are trapped. Salmon (1998) uses this term, and the following is an adaptation of his description of 'nodal' points in the web.

The web is constantly changing – shrinking or expanding. Short periods of relative poverty, for example, can often be weathered by using savings or borrowing from other members of the family or friends, but long-term poverty can generate all sorts of additional problems – debt, denial of access to financial services, loss of dignity, homelessness – with the result that people are drawn ever more tightly into the web. Some things are particularly likely to trigger the process, and we will remind ourselves of these below. But in areas with a long history of deprivation, children are born into the condition of social exclusion. Just as areas of deprivation are a product of wider economic and social forces, so individuals are shaped by the conditions into which they are born. There is a link between the global, the neighbourhood and the individual.

And yet it is because social exclusion has many facets that it lends itself to intervention by a variety of agencies co-operating in order to provide 'joined-up' responses. It is in this context that community development has a valuable contribution to make. By working with local people it can enable them to respond to problems which are capable of being resolved locally. It may also enable them to exert pressure for wider changes that cannot be delivered through intervention at the neighbourhood or wider level.

One of the positive things to emerge from the SEU's 2001 report is that there is now an undertaking to finance this kind of intervention on a scale not previously experienced. In this sense, the climate is favourable for community development.

Material factors
Income and poverty
A report on poverty and social exclusion indicates that at the end of 1999 '... a quarter of the British population was living in poverty, measured in terms of low income and multiple deprivation of necessities' (Joseph Rowntree Foundation, 2000, p1). 'Necessities' in prosperous societies

embrace items which fall outside any absolute definition of poverty, but being unable to afford them reinforces the process of exclu*sion. Cary Oppenheim points out that though there is considerable movement at the bottom of the income scale, it is often of a 'revolving door' kind: 'Although people in poverty do move from the bottom rung of the ladder, a large proportion do not move very far' (Oppenheim, 1998, p16). Poverty has a ratchet effect, and inadequate income over a long period triggers other aspects of social exclusion.

Poverty also often means that access to financial services is denied. One in five people has no bank account, and many live in areas from which building societies and banks have withdrawn. Shops and service providers are often 'postcode' sensitive. Local shops may be few and expensive. People often have to cash their cheques and giros at the new breed of money shops. If the neighbourhood lacks a credit union, then the poor are often driven into the hands of ruthless money lenders charging extortionate rates of interest. The tax free saving measures introduced by a succession of chancellors do nothing for the poorest.

Blair's commitment to 'eradicate child poverty' by 2019 is welcome and necessary. A report by UNICEF researchers for the Institute of Public Policy Research (Micklewright and Stewart, 2000) shows that the UK comes bottom of the European Union league on three out of five criteria used by the authors. It also shows that nearly 20 per cent of young people live in households beneath the official poverty line of household income – below half median earnings.

Unemployment

One of Labour's clearest and firmest commitments was to tackle unemployment, particularly that experienced by younger adults and by older workers, who were the most likely to experience long-term unemployment. Labour also willed the means for doing this. Though the government inherited a downward trend in unemployment and was helped by a buoyant economy, it nevertheless recognised that many of those who continued to be unemployed would be among the socially excluded. The debate about the degree of effectiveness achieved by the New Deal will continue, but the Chancellor's willingness to refer to the importance of achieving full employment – leaving aside how that is to be defined in today's economy – has been a welcome change after the dominance of monetarist notions that unemployment is necessary to control both unions and inflation.

Although short periods of unemployment do not necessarily lock people into a web of social exclusion, longer periods – particularly where there is only one breadwinner – can be economically and socially devastating. For older people it can affect their sense of worth and lead to illness, and for younger people – particularly those from homes where unemployment is a generational experience – it can lead to the development of a sub-culture. In many of the neighbourhood renewal areas unemployment has remained stubbornly high in spite of the measures taken to get people into employment. If the Chancellor's commitment to full employment is to be realised, work will have to be created in the voluntary and public sectors, at least in the short term.

Housing and environment

Approximately 9.5 million people are unable to afford adequate housing conditions. Housing and the environment are two of the most obvious indicators of neighbourhood deprivation. Until Thatcher's government adopted a policy of selling off council housing to tenants at subsidised prices, such housing was the domain of a broad band of working class people, most of whom had steady jobs and a reasonable standard of living. However, now that much of the best council housing has become owner-occupied, we find that the remaining social housing is occupied by couples with low incomes, single parents or older people. This also affects the next generation who, unlike children whose parents are owner-occupiers, will not benefit from the inheritance of a property. This further widens the inequalities in society, particularly in wealthy suburban areas.

Social housing and a poor environment often go together. Outer urban areas often have poor transport, few shops and inadequate social amenities. Vandalism and – possibly – high levels of crime, together with security measures, inadequate lighting and a general appearance of decay add to a sense of despair. In older inner city areas, the environment will often be affected by traffic, inadequate parking facilities, pollution, unsightly workshops and warehouses.

Disability and chronic illness

In the 1960s the Office of Population Censuses and Surveys (OPCS) identified impairment, disability and handicap as different categories. Townsend (1979) added chronic ill-health. These conditions do not necessarily lead to poverty or result in social exclusion, but Alcock (1997) points out that in the1960s OPCS calculated that 47 per cent of people with disabilities were experiencing poverty. Experts in this field maintain that state benefits are the main source of income for disabled people. It must also be borne in mind that more than half are outside the labour market because of age.

There can be no quarrel with a policy that involves necessary health checks so long as these are carried out with sensitivity, nor with the government's desire to enable more people with disabilities or suffering from some form of chronic illness to move into suitable employment. Even part-time employment can help provide links to mainstream society and increase people's feeling of self-worth. However, in order to make this possible, action will be required to combat discrimination and improve access to transport and buildings. The strengthening of the Disability Commission and the New Deal for people with disabilities are to be welcomed.

Crime

Anti-social behaviour – the preferred phrase for the SEU's work on crime – is more prevalent in deprived neighbourhoods and, according to the PAT 9 report, appears to be increasing. It is recognised that it can be fuelled by other problems associated with social exclusion such as poverty, unemployment, school truancy and suspensions. For some, burglary, mugging and drug dealing are seen as ways of surviving on low state incomes. Even children in their early teens are now 'serving an apprenticeship' in small-scale drug trading.

Crime and fear of it can deepen the sense of loneliness and isolation of some of the most vulnerable people living in high crime neighbourhoods. Apart from the emotional consequences of a burglary, there is the added problem that contents insurance is costly in such areas and therefore many people have no cover.

Discrimination

As the SEU's report points out, minority ethnic groups are likely to be disproportionately represented in the population of deprived areas (SEU, 2000b). They are also more likely than others to be poor and unemployed, suffer ill-health and live in the least popular housing. For them crime also involves a well founded fear of racial harassment. The statistical evidence is damning. It shows the extent to which minority ethnic groups are concentrated in the 44 most deprived local authority areas in the country, and how they are at a disadvantage in both employment and income compared with equivalent white groups.

There are significant differences between minority ethnic groups, with Pakistanis and Bangladeshis coming out worst in tables on household income, unemployment and educational attainment. Indians fare much better on most criteria. Black people still appear to suffer discrimination in terms of the criminal justice system.

The SEU is making laudable recommendations on the way in which some of the issues can be addressed. Yet, at the same time, the government operates a system of vouchers for asylum seekers that can only be spent on necessities while their cases are pending. This is degrading and militates against promoting any sense of inclusion.

Gender plays a part in the experience of social exclusion. Single mothers are over represented in social housing, and women in deprived areas often bear a particularly heavy burden. Even in two-parent households they are usually left to manage essential household expenditure on a low income, deal with children and – if possible – get a job which will probably be low paid. There has been no attempt to recognise the economic value of care work, a point which is emphasised by Levitas (op. cit., pp61-63) and Lister (op. cit.).

Leisure and transport

The limitations which poor people experience in both leisure and transport are another consequence of exclusion. Nearly 7.5 million people cannot afford leisure activities such as theme parks, sports events and holidays.

The poor can be disadvantaged in respect of transport in two ways. Car ownership in deprived areas invariably falls well below the average for their town or city – as it does in many rural areas. For example, in 1991 in Hillfields, 64 per cent of households had no car, compared with a national average of 32.4 per cent. Also, many deprived outer estates have poor public transport facilities, and residents in inner city areas often suffer both high levels of pollution and danger for pedestrians, particularly older people and children.

This has not been a comprehensive review of the different interrelated components in a web of social exclusion. There are other factors (for example, family breakdown, debt, a prison record, mental illness, lack of education), but we have drawn attention to some of the things most likely to lead to an intensification of the experience of exclusion.

Psycho-social aspects

Because the process is dynamic, it is not always possible to distinguish between those factors that deepen the experience and those that are the consequences of it. The government is right to point out that lack of educational qualifications reduces the chances of employment, but educational failure may also be partly due to a lack of motivation arising out of living in a milieu where schooling is regarded as a burden. This is especially the case when we turn to socio-psychological factors. However, we will first look at the consequences for health in general.

Health

A link between social exclusion and some aspects of health is widely accepted. However, the relationship is not as simple as was originally thought. Sloggett and Joshi (1994) tracked 300,000 people selected randomly from the 1981 census and traced their mortality rates over nearly nine years. Their research showed that mortality rates were consistently higher amongst deprived people, but these remained consistent whether people lived in or out of a deprived area.

In his major study Wilkinson (1996), drawing upon research in different parts of the world, found that though absolute poverty clearly affects health, after an adequate income is achieved social factors come into play – including powerlessness (see below). Long-term studies based upon areas as diverse as a small town in eastern America and countries in eastern Europe have led Wilkinson and others to conclude that levels of inequality and the consequent degree of social cohesion in societies have implications for people's psychological, emotional and social wellbeing. He draws attention to a study in America which reinforces the evidence for a causal link between social cohesion and mortality (Kawachi et al. 1996). The Medical Officer for Health drew attention to the affects of inequality for health in this country, referring in particular to rises in the death rate for unskilled men since the early 1970s (Acheson, 1998). In February 2001 the Minister of Health announced ten-year targets for reducing infant mortality and reducing premature adult deaths. This clearly has implications for the government's programme to combat social exclusion.

Sense of isolation

While the term social exclusion is used by professionals, it is not normally used by the socially excluded themselves. Donnison (1998) prefers to talk about poverty and inequality, and opts for words such as pain, hardship and suffering to describe how exclusion is experienced. On outer urban estates and in former coalfield communities residents refer to feeling cut off, isolated and forgotten, and in blighted inner city areas they are likely to talk about 'living in fear' or a 'ghetto', and being 'treated like rubbish'.

Unemployment, together with a lack of money, limits opportunities for making wider social contacts. People are trapped in a small world. And yet at the same time, through advertising and television images, they are taunted by consumer goods and life styles which can only become theirs by winning the Lottery.

Alienation

People's sense of alienation expresses itself in various ways. One is in a deep sense of separateness from the institutions of society. We have made reference to the way in which some groups show little interest in education. This is particularly the case with many marginalised white people, and with second and third generation African Caribbean families. It is reflected in truancy and school exclusion figures. On the other hand, some minority ethnic groups – notably Indians – place a great emphasis on education and the benefits it can bring.

There is considerable suspicion of the institutions of law and order in some areas and – not surprisingly – this is particularly the case in black communities, and is one of the reasons why targets for the recruitment of police officers from minority ethnic groups are not being achieved. Though there is a wider cultural change taking place in the way in which traditional authority figures such as priests, officials, politicians, teachers and police are regarded, this attitude is most apparent in deprived areas.

Alienation is also seen in the way in which people in deprived areas rarely participate in political and democratic processes. Turnout in some poorer wards in the last local elections was as low as 13 per cent. The point can be sharply illustrated from the 1997 General Election. In the impoverished Riverside constituency in Liverpool the turnout was only 51.9 per cent, but across the Mersey in an affluent Wirral constituency it was 81 per cent. This is related to another dominant feeling of the excluded.

Powerlessness

The low turnouts at all elections, particularly in the most deprived wards, is largely a consequence of people's sense of powerlessness. Those who have had a long experience of being excluded from mainstream society do not feel that they have a stake in the political system. This is reinforced by an electoral emphasis on marginal constituencies and middle England, and by the composition of the constitutional bodies which represent us. Even Labour members of Parliament are predominantly drawn from professional groups, and the 'working class' member is now almost a figure from the past. The same is true when you look at the composition of non-elected bodies – such as quangos and National Health Trusts – which now play such an influential part in determining the kind of society in which we live.

Kenneth Galbraith voiced his concern about America's 'democracy of the contented and comfortable' (Galbraith, 1993, p155). Only around 40 per cent of the electorate vote and those who do are mainly the prosperous. If 'the poor resorted reliably to the ballot box to redress their ills the politicians would eagerly solicit their votes by presenting policies which addressed their needs' (Galbraith, 1996, p139). But it is a self-perpetuating problem. The excluded have felt so powerless for so long that they do not see any point in voting. Survival is their object, not participation in politics. And in this country, focus groups in middle England are hardly likely to reduce this sense of powerlessness. The problem indicates the importance of the concept of 'stakeholding'. Those who have had a long and often inter-generational experience of having no stake in society are not likely to be quickly or easily empowered. Powerlessness reduces people's sense of self-worth and can have a debilitating effect on health.

Social exclusion and policy

In the previous sections we have described social exclusion, broken it down into the elements which contribute to it and have referred to several of the positive ways in which the government is seeking to tackle it. Its neighbourhood strategy is more ambitious, comprehensive and carefully worked out than any previous attempt to deal with neighbourhood deprivation. Nevertheless, some commentators have expressed reservations about its ability to realise its overarching aim. We share some of these.

The problems being tackled have a long history. They go back more than the 20 years referred to in the SEU's reports, though it is true that during this period they were exacerbated by policies which led to greater inequality and global economic changes. However, it was recognised in the late 1960s that the achievements of the welfare state had not succeeded in eliminating poverty, and it was this realisation that prompted the Urban Programme, Education Priority Areas and CDPs at the end of the 1960s.

In the web of social exclusion, poverty usually leads to other forms of exclusion. Health, crime, educational attainment and powerlessness are frequently affected by income. If we accept the validity of some of the research referred to by Wilkinson (op. cit.), the vast gap between rich and poor in society, which widened between 1970 and 1999, has a negative effect on social cohesion and health.

From the beginning, the government's social exclusion strategy has been located within a programme of:

- Targeting additional financial help on 'deserving' groups such as the poorest pensioners, children and working families whose income falls beneath the poverty level.
- Promoting equal opportunities through education and establishing programmes such as New Deal and Welfare To Work, aimed at getting people into employment.
- Other modest redistributive measures.

Though this strategy is commendable as far as it goes, it leaves out those people left behind in the expanding job market because they live in the wrong areas or have limitations which are not easily remedied through education and training, and others who depend upon inadequate benefits. At the cost of extending means-testing, the position with regard to pensioners is being much improved, but until the basic pension is again linked to earnings, there is unlikely to be a permanent reduction in income inequality for senior citizens.

One of the prime purposes of strategies to combat social exclusion is to generate a greater sense of social cohesion, but in order to achieve this there needs to be a commitment to creating a more egalitarian society. Lister (op. cit.) supports the view that redistributive measures through the tax-benefit system are a necessary component of creating a more inclusive society. They encourage a sense of reciprocity and of common citizenship between the very comfortable and those who live in relative poverty. This supports our view that 'Bringing Britain Together' will require redistribution at a national level as well as intervention at the neighbourhood level. Secondly, though we have highlighted the very positive features of social exclusion, it is capable of being interpreted in different ways and sometimes given a negative connotation. Earlier in this chapter we noted that government ministers move uneasily between different interpretations of the term. The final paragraph of the SEU's National Strategy for Neighbourhood Renewal calls for proof that the big vision can work.

> *But proving that the Strategy can work goes deeper than analysing the logic of its institutions or proving that it would get money to the right areas. It is the more fundamental question of whether the most disadvantaged people and places can ever change.*
>
> (SEU, 2000a, p90, authors' emphasis)

This statement of the 'big vision' is tantalising because of its narrow focus. It appears to place the burden of proof on disadvantaged people, and could be regarded as implying a 'pathology' model of individuals and communities. Increasingly – as in Scotland – there is a preference for social inclusion because it embraces the rich as well as the poor and is more positive.

Finally, it should be noted that the track record of geographically targeted initiatives (GTIs) is not good. The anecdotal illustration of Hillfields is an example, but it is also supported by Robson *et al.* (1994) who estimated that between 1979 and 1991 a total of about £9.3 billion was spent on such initiatives. Howarth and colleagues conclude that there is little evidence that GTIs have done much to alleviate poverty (Joseph Rowntree

Foundation, 1999). The conclusion of Root (2000), on the basis of her local government based research, appears to be that GTIs will continue to constitute a major part in tackling social exclusion and therefore should be used as positively as possible.

Exclusion, inclusion and community development

So far the stress has been on social exclusion and, by inference, achieving inclusion. The next two chapters will deal with community development in relation to these two concepts. Here we will comment on three inter-related points which arise out of the study of the SEU's publications – in particular the report of PAT 9 dealing with community self-help (Home Office, 1999).

The first is that while PAT 9 distinguishes between neighbourhood and community, the distinction becomes increasingly blurred. Even though there is an understanding of some of the marks of community, frequently it is used as though it represents a cohesive or homogenous whole. Field research in America and France (Wacquant, 1996) has shown that many of the neighbourhoods where the socially excluded are concentrated are highly disorganised. The same can be said of many deprived neighbourhoods in this country.

Even in those neighbourhoods where there are strong social networks and community groups, these may not be broadly based or representative of those who are most excluded. Without a detailed knowledge of a neighbourhood, agencies are unlikely to be fully aware of the local dynamics. Are there partially concealed conflicts of interest? To what extent are some people 'excluded' by those who are less caught up in the web? How widely are people in groups representative of the area? How are people selected or elected for partnership bodies?

Secondly, there is the danger of a mechanistic approach towards 'communities'. This is most clearly displayed in PAT 9's recommendation of targets for levels of participation, starting with a baseline and setting targets for the following years. There are usually few formalised groups in deprived areas, and those which do exist are rarely made up of the most excluded. Field experience suggests that such information in an accurate form would be difficult to collect, and even more difficult to maintain over a lengthy period. Statistical record keeping usually ranks low in the concerns of community groups: many are informal, some are short-life and most are struggling with the task in hand. Information about the composition of groups in terms of gender, ethnicity and socio-economic status of its participants and about the group's goals and achievements would be valuable. But who would be responsible for assembling this information?

25

Community development appreciates the importance of assessing outcomes, and evaluation should always be a feature of practice. Because it is about a process, workers recognise the importance of qualitative research into outcomes, but the practical difficulties associated with both quantitative and qualitative research are considerable. We return to this topic later.

There is a tendency to overestimate people's desire, willingness or time for participation. Research into the pilot projects for Better Government for Older People and for Best Value show that though the majority of people felt that they should be consulted, only a tiny minority were prepared to become actively engaged in the process. Researchers note that people's 'unwillingness to become involved stems in part from their belief that it will not result in tangible improvements in services or in their quality of life' (Martin and Boaz, 2000, p51). There is no reason to believe that reactions will be more positive in many deprived neighbourhoods.

Our third point is that while the community self-help report contains perceptive comments and suggestions, it appears too idealistic about what can be achieved. In support of self-help, chapter 2 of the report describes several useful and apparently successful projects, but experience suggests that one needs to look carefully at the background of those who are involved and also to consider whether the project is likely to deliver a consistent service over a long period. It is usually the most excluded who are least likely to be involved.

West and McCormick (1998) provide a valuable contribution by applying a micro-economic strategy to the task of developing social inclusion, though they stress that 'vertical' links are also necessary. This is probably one of the most justified and constructive approaches to self-help. But even then, we must be careful not to build up unreal expectations. For example, both West and McCormick and the PAT 9 report mention food cooperatives and local exchange trading schemes (LETS) as ways in which people in deprived neighbourhoods can improve their situations. Yet LETS frequently fail to engage those who would benefit most from their activities. This is not an argument against any self-help initiative, only a plea for realism.

Community development is concerned with promoting a sense of inclusion. Self-help can assist, but it must be an activity freely undertaken by local people, often with the support of an experienced community worker. The SEU recognises that this is only part of the 'joined-up' solution, but it can make a contribution to the process. It is important, however, that it does not become an expectation that the socially excluded should provide services which people in prosperous areas would either demand or purchase.

3 Mapping the connections

Two key themes in community development are the fact that it is predominately rooted in neighbourhoods – engaging local people through direct, face-to-face contact – and its concern to influence regional, national and international policies, using the commitment and energy of local action to campaign for changes in systems and policies that influence the lives of people in poverty so profoundly. The two themes permeate the experiences of community development, both historically and today.

This chapter has two purposes. One is to draw out the connections between community development and anti-poverty or social inclusion work. The other is to examine the theoretical basis of the connections and suggest the implications of an historical, contemporary and theoretical analysis for policymakers and for community development itself. It is important to note the latter aspect of the discussion because it is as necessary to ask tough questions of community development as a professional intervention in the context of social exclusion as it is of government and other agencies.

There is a dearth of studies looking at the relationship between community development and social inclusion initiatives. While the focus of this booklet is on this relationship, it is important to make clear that we are not suggesting that community development can achieve social inclusion by itself. We argued in the previous chapter the need for programmes at the 'micro' level to be part of 'macro' policy changes impacting on inequality and social injustice. Here we wish to emphasise that, at area and neighbourhood levels, community development is only one component in social inclusion programmes. Claims made for community development should not be misinterpreted as suggesting panaceas. This mistake, as we shall see in the following historical summary, has dogged community development in the past.

Historical survey
United States
Debate on the motivation of President Johnson for declaring, in his first State of the Union message (1964), a 'war on poverty', continues to this day. Looking back at this turbulent period in America's history one is struck by the combination of confidence and naivete with which politicians and administrators called for the 'maximum feasible participation' of the poor in the war on poverty. Commentators have noted how policy-

makers quickly sought to put the cork in the bottle of the genie they had unleashed: 'There is little doubt that one of the main aims in devising the Model Cities Program was to reverse some of the policies enshrined in the Economic Opportunity Act and restore control of federal monies at a local level to the Mayor and City Hall' (Higgins, 1978, p34). The Model Cities Program was a planning mechanism enabling residents and community leaders to have dialogue with city officials. A study of the programme reported very mixed results (Brager and Specht, 1973, pp52-3).

The effect of making such a close connection between poverty and community action in the US did not, however, disappear so rapidly, despite the changed context and circumstance in the 1970s and 1980s. Organisers were aware of the need to sustain the connection even though they were operating in a hard and defensive context. As much attention was given to the process of organising as to the content: 'It means working realistically, working with and respecting the personal and political strengths and limitations of our members and organisations as they are and not as we wish them to be' (Burghardt, 1982, p14).

Even in the next decade, when the various traditions of community action and community organising in the US were dwarfed by the forward march of community enterprise, we can observe the concern to maintain the link between participation and anti-poverty work. The strong interest shown by researchers and policymakers in the concept of social capital – the networks and trust between people that can be highly significant in building strong communities – also addresses the link. Commenting on the work of Robert Putnam on social capital (1993, 1995), two researchers refer to 'a virtual industry of interest and action created around the implications of his findings for the development of low-income communities' (Gittel and Vidal, 1998, p14).

UK and Europe

Taking experiences from the US and making use of them in the UK has been as evident in the community development and poverty sectors as it has elsewhere. In 1969, British experts involved in the Educational Priority Area programme participated in an international conference, the main objective of which was learning lessons from American experiences. Those involved in designing the more high profile Community Development Projects (referred to in chapter 1) were clearly influenced by the American anti-poverty programmes. They met with American counterparts to fine-tune the British programme. The 12 areas in which CDP operated were chosen to include several different types. All, however, experienced various forms of economic and social deprivation so that once again, in the UK equivalent of the American war on poverty, we can see a clear link being made between community participation and anti-poverty work. CDP's structural analysis of deprivation, with its message that local action alone could not tackle problems, was a major influence on the thinking of community workers and others.

In the 1970s, community development expanded and the connections between community development and anti-poverty work were less evident. The links had been made rather more clearly by community development workers than by the poverty lobby. During the 1980s and 1990s, however, despite the defensive stance forced upon community development by the Thatcher government, the connection began to be re-established, notably in the anti-poverty strategies of local authorities (Pearson *et al.*, 1997). Furthermore, community development organisations themselves sought to commit community development to a stance which aligned it to working in deprived communities and to involving those people who were excluded from democratic and participatory processes. The opening statement in the charter of the Standing Conference for Community Development reads: 'Community development is crucially concerned with the issues of powerlessness and disadvantage; as such it should involve all members of society, and offers a practice that is part of a process of social change' (SCCD, 1992), and its new strategic framework for community development cites as a commitment 'Prioritising the issues of concern to people experiencing poverty and social exclusion' (SCCD, 2001, p5). A similar emphasis is evident in documentation from the Scottish Community Development Centre: the first statement of community development values identified is 'combating social exclusion, poverty and disadvantage and discrimination' (Barr and Hashagen, 2000, p52).

It can be seen, therefore, that both the history and policy statements of community development in the UK contain a strong anti-poverty element. The two areas cannot be equated – some community development does not have this element. As we discussed in chapter 2, the advantage of the concept of social exclusion is that it helps us to see the multiple dimensions of exclusion and the combined impact of these dimensions on a given individual, family or community. The critical question, which we address in the next chapter, is how this 'tradition' might transfer into implementation of the government's policy aimed at combating social exclusion.

The wider European context is also significant. We referred in the previous chapter to the third European Anti-Poverty Programme, which was particularly significant in terms of providing evidence to the European Union of the importance of citizen participation. A number of other EU programmes subsequently encouraged community development, notably RECHAR in former coalfield communities and LEADER, the rural development programme. In his analysis of social inclusion and citizenship in the European context, Henderson argues that, despite the differences of context and environment across Europe, there are shared experiences of social exclusion, notably as an attack on human dignity aligned with a sense of powerlessness: 'The principles on which community development is based and which inform the thinking and action of excluded people are relevant to every kind of poor community – inner city, peripheral estate, former mining villages, sparsely populated rural areas' (Henderson, 1997, p10). There are also examples in other European countries of community development being used as a key component of a social inclusion strategy, notably in Ireland. European networks such as the European Anti-Poverty Network and the Combined European Bureau for Social Development have helped to disseminate examples of good practice.

Southern countries

Parallel with the UK and European community development traditions, development agencies based in the rich countries of the North have been working with community-based organisations in the South to support participatory approaches to grassroots development: 'Along with 'empowerment', 'participation' and 'gender-equity', capacity building is seen as an essential element if development is to be sustainable and centred in people' (Eade, 1997, p1). Capacity-building and sustainable development represent a new phase, historically, in the use of community development principles and methods in the South, a very different phase to that led by the UK and other colonial powers and the United Nations in an earlier era.

Interest in making connections between northern and southern countries on the issue of community participation has grown considerably in recent years. Oxfam, for example, set up an anti-poverty programme for Britain and Ireland and has supported exchanges between community groups and encouraged use of techniques such as participatory action research which have been developed primarily in the South. Similarly, there is interest in development agencies in learning from the North: 'We can learn a great deal about the use of participation to address poverty and social exclusion by looking at how the concept has been used in the North, where policies to promote participation for community development and poverty alleviation have been tried for several decades' (Gaventa, 1998, p50).

The above synoptic historical survey demonstrates the extent to which community development has been linked, at policy level, with the issue of social exclusion. Whether community development has delivered results is a different and equally important question. Here we are simply alerting the reader to the variety of connections which have been made between the two concepts throughout the history of community development.

Contemporary context

Community development faces a new challenge on how it connects with social exclusion. The following scan of how government policies, local authorities, health authorities and voluntary organisations are seeking to engage with the issue of social exclusion via community development and participation highlights the need to clarify what community development can contribute to social inclusion strategies and programmes.

Government policies

The SEU's reports on neighbourhood renewal have, as we saw in the introductory chapter, a strong emphasis on community involvement. Already plans are being made to take forward some of the recommendations contained in the reports of the 18 Policy Action Teams (PATs) and many of these have major implications for community development. In Scotland, the Scottish Community Development Centre is undertaking a large-scale training programme for staff and local people involved in the Scottish Executive's Social Inclusion Partnership. In England, the government's Neighbourhood Renewal Strategy is being taken forward by the Department of Transport, Local Government and the Regions (DTLR). Even before the details of its long-term strategy for combating social exclusion are finalised, the government appears to be in a hurry to get things moving on the community involvement front.

One problem for the government is how to weld the ideas and programmes emerging from the SEU with other, on-going programmes. This applies especially to the regeneration field, as the then DETR continued to ensure that local authorities and others bidding for government funding under the Single Regeneration Budget (SRB) take seriously the issue of community involvement. This insistence was reinforced in 1998 with the setting up of regional development agencies (RDAs): 'In their initial development strategies, many RDAs have identified scope for involving organisations from the voluntary and community sectors in local and subregional partnerships. These are particularly aimed at regeneration and social inclusion objectives' (Chanan, Gilchrist and West, 1999, p5). Since then, however, the emphasis by RDAs on community involvement has lessened. There are signs that they will increasingly concentrate on physical development.

Through its New Deal for Communities programme, which is located in the poorest neighbourhoods, the government has been able to test out some of the approaches being taken forward by the SEU. Similarly, the Home Office's Active Communities Unit, which has funded national community development organisations for a number of years, has accumulated wide-ranging experience on which the SEU's strategy should be able to build.

The Local Government Act 2000 places on principal local authorities a duty to prepare community strategies, and the DETR issued guidance which identifies four essential objectives of a community strategy that will need to be met:

- Allow local communities (based upon geography and/or interest) to articulate their aspirations, needs and priorities.

- Co-ordinate the actions of the council, and of the public, private, voluntary and community organisations that operate locally.

- Focus and shape existing and future activity of those organisations so that they effectively meet community needs and aspirations.

- Contribute to the achievement of sustainable development.

(DETR, 2000b)

CDF has published parallel guidance (Chanan, Garratt and West, 2000). This is the latest in a series of measures and initiatives coming from the DETR and other government departments which seek to engage with local communities. The Department for Education and Skills' Sure Start and its Neighbourhood Support Fund are two further examples. While not all the initiatives have an explicit link with social exclusion, there is a common message encouraging community involvement, particularly in poor neighbourhoods.

There is, in addition, the European dimension – regeneration programmes in the UK which depend upon European Union funding. For the period 2000-2006, social inclusion will be a more explicit theme for the deployment of the Structural Funds, and between 1997 and 2000, capacity building became, experimentally, part of the European Social Fund. As we have seen, other EU programmes have supported community development. For example, a report on the EU-funded Peace Programme in Northern Ireland states: 'Community development as a change process offers an approach which can address inclusion from the bottom up, embracing inclusion as both a means and an end. It is characterised by multi-dimensionality, partnership and participation' (Northern Ireland Voluntary Trust, 1999a, p3).

Local authorities

The reform of local government being pursued by the government is ensuring that local authorities turn their attention more thoroughly than most have done in the past to working in partnership with communities. Best Value and Community Strategies are two key initiatives in this context. Plans for Local Strategic Partnerships place a similar emphasis on the importance of community involvement.

At the same time, local authorities are continuing their commitment to having Local Agenda 21 and anti-poverty strategies, many of which contain a strong community involvement element. The momentum built up within local authorities on this issue is being channelled into the new social inclusion agenda. As a result, increasing numbers of authorities are seeing the need to have community development strategies: on the one hand there clearly has to be 'joined-up' thinking and action on issues across a local authority, on the other the authority has to have meaningful ways of engaging with communities. Community development is crucial on both counts. The following is an example of a local authority which has recently made a new commitment to community development.

**Durham County Council:
Community development strategy and action plan**

In adopting this policy for community development the County Council agrees to engage individuals and groups on a genuine participatory basis, which will demonstrate commitment to encouraging participation in the democratic process, particularly those communities who are most socially excluded and disadvantaged.

Four strategic objectives flow from the policy. These are:

* Improving community governance.
* Tackling social exclusion.
* Improving partnerships.
* Building community capacity.

(Durham County Council, 1999, p2)

There is ample evidence to demonstrate that local authorities, through their own initiatives or as a result of government requirements, are heavily involved in connecting community development and social exclusion.

Health authorities/departments

The government's aim to improve health and well-being and reduce health inequalities requires health authorities and health departments to assess the health needs of their populations and develop a Health Improvement Programme. Increasing numbers of Primary Care Groups are developing a community development approach, and Health Action Zones have been active in advocating community development.

This new policy emphasis builds on wide-ranging experiences of community development within a health context and there is now a considerable body of knowledge on good practice. Much of the current interest has a strong link to social exclusion: 'Inequalities are a central concern of community development approaches to health' (Hashagen, 1998, p8).

Voluntary organisations

It is impossible to generalise about the connections between community development and social exclusion across all voluntary organisations. What we can see, however, is how organisations involved in social inclusion work have sought to include this dimension and how those involved in community development have engaged with social exclusion. Two examples in the first category are the Poverty Alliance in Scotland and the Church Urban Fund in England, both of which have a strong commitment to supporting local community involvement in anti-poverty initiatives. Two examples in the second category are the British Association of Settlements and Social Action Centres and the Standing Conference for Community Development – representative bodies, drawing together local, regional and national organisations. Both have urged the SEU to ensure that the National Strategy for Neighbourhood Renewal takes community involvement seriously, arguing that otherwise local people will not be active participants.

Many other voluntary organisations go out of their way to demonstrate the necessary links between social inclusion and community development, with the churches and childcare organisations such as Barnardo's and the Children's Society having considerable experience in this field. The UK Coalition on Poverty, through its Voices for Change project, is giving a new impetus to this approach. We have seen how development agencies such as Oxfam and Save the Children operate within this framework, as do European organisations such as the European Anti-Poverty Network.

Overall, therefore, the contemporary context lends weight to the government's conviction that a neighbourhood-based social inclusion strategy will work. The next question we ask is, what are the key ideas that lie behind community development's commitment to combating social exclusion which enable it to claim effectiveness in this territory?

Theory

Central to community development thinking is its robust determination to counter assumptions that poor people must depend on services from welfare agencies, that they lack the motivation and skills to do things for themselves. Community development has been explicit about making exclusion and disadvantage a priority. It is the commitment to working with the most disadvantaged and oppressed groups in society that explains why there is an emphasis in community development on supporting women, members of minority ethnic groups and unemployed people. Groups most at risk of poverty are those which are also most likely to experience discrimination.

Some commentators have felt that community development has become trapped as a result of its focus on disadvantage. They see it as being used as a strategy of last resort in neighbourhoods which are fragmenting: deteriorating environment, high unemployment, vandalism, experience and fear of crime, latent violence. As a result, the external causes of poverty and disadvantage are not addressed. In its most extreme form, this use of community development can be interpreted as a way of 'cooling out' protest. Alternatively, community development lays itself open to severe criticism because of its alleged failure to deliver:

> In areas of extreme poverty, where socialist and trade union traditions are weak, local community groups are bound to prove difficult to organize and, over any length of time, even harder to sustain. The poor have good reason to view representatives of the welfare state with deep suspicion, even when appearing in the apparently friendly guise of community worker.
>
> (Jacobs, 1994, p169)

Partly in response to these criticisms, advocates of community development have redoubled their efforts to ensure that they operate at policy levels – within government, local government and other agencies – as well as at the local, neighbourhood level. Inevitably this approach is informed by contrasting ideologies. One, picking up the CDP analysis, holds that the causes of poverty and disaffection are structural, not lodged in the pathology or supposedly inherent weaknesses of particular neighbourhoods.

Another bases its approach on an effectiveness argument: only by working with the intent of influencing policies will meaningful change be achieved.

Running alongside these broader theoretical issues is community development theory concerned with application. It rests on a concept of participation that challenges any evidence of cliques or individuals dominating a group and which seeks to keep opportunities for participation open. This speaks to our theme of community development's focus on the participation of people in poverty, especially those who are least likely to attend public meetings, join a demonstration or sit on a committee.

Concern about who participates, and at what kind of level, has been ongoing in community development and explains the widespread use made of the 'ladder of participation' (Arnstein, 1969), which illustrates the different ways in which organisations can approach participation and consultation, ranging from non-participation and tokenism to full citizen power. The assumption – rightly so – is that community development will always resist programmes or activities which appear to treat residents' involvement in a tokenistic way. It cannot be assumed that community development's definition of participation is the same as definitions used in government, local authority and health programmes.

Some of community development's potential to contribute to struggles for social inclusion is to be found in its methods, skills and knowledge base: the process of building confidence and mutual trust within a group; the skills of working with people who are angry, depressed and often alienated from mainstream society; the knowledge of how particular communities work – the leaders, opinion-makers and informal networks. We return to this key area in chapter 4. At this point, however, it is important to draw attention to the other key area where community development connects with social inclusion: the benefits and services that it can provide. Each of the following represents a particular way in which community development can engage with social exclusion.

Local organisations and structures

The core of community development practices is about helping people to set up autonomous community groups and supporting their involvement in other structures such as community forums and partnerships. Grassroots organisations make it possible for the socially excluded to be heard. There are, of course, other ways of doing this – the Poverty Hearings organised by Church Action on Poverty on a city-wide basis is one example; the Commission on Poverty, Participation and Power another – but locally-based groups have the advantage of being accessible and, arguably, less threatening arenas in which poor people can become involved. This means that community groups must be willing to involve such people – and this is where the role of the community worker can be crucial – insisting that cliques of local people do not put up barriers to the participation of people who are perceived to be different.

A distinctive characteristic of community development is its capacity to reduce the separateness of groups and organisations. At community level this can mean that 'categories' of people who are socially excluded – such as pensioners, the low paid, women, travellers and minority ethnic groups – have the possibility of joining together. Each group faces particular problems yet they all share experiences of exclusion. This kind of unifying work is not easy and the skills and patience of a community worker are usually essential if the different groups are to function together effectively.

Reduced prices/increased quality

Finding ways of purchasing affordable, good quality food can be crucial for poor people. Becoming involved in a food co-operative can be an effective way of achieving these objectives.

Food co-operatives are run and controlled by local people. Usually, however, they require good support from local professionals such as health workers and community workers. To be successful, food co-operatives need to be organised and managed very carefully. Organisations running them can be flexible about when to make goods accessible. Some co-ops favour mobile shops. Many have contributed to health education courses in schools and health centres.

Increasing incomes

Advice and information services can be provided in communities, which can result in increasing the income of poor people. The services do not have to be thought of only in service delivery terms: they can link to community issues and be supported by local people. In addition, welfare rights campaigns can use a number of methods, including articles in local and community newspapers, posters, use of local radio and resource centres, to bring to the attention of people in poverty their rights to state benefits.

The combination of targeted information on benefits with community participation methods has been found to be very effective. Bob Holman, describing the work of Fare, a community project in Easterhouse, Glasgow, has highlighted the advantages of the combination:

> *As Fare's participants are familiar with life at the hard end, those in need can turn to us as understanding friends, not distant officials. When some members knew that a low-paid couple were taking in a child of a neighbour*

serving a prison sentence, they suggested, in confidence, that a grant might be possible. Fare also ensures that grants can be accompanied by other forms of support

(*The Guardian*, 28 February 2001)

Promoting collaboration

Local people can agree to support and join organisations whose aim is to help poor people and deprived neighbourhoods to have improved access to services, resources and employment. People on low incomes frequently become victims of high charges for credit. Credit unions are self-help financial co-operatives. As a result of living in the same neighbourhood or belonging to the same organisation (a 'common bond'), people agree to support a credit union and contribute modest amounts on a regular basis. In return, they can obtain low-cost loans.

Community enterprise

Projects designed to combat unemployment and poverty through various forms of employment-related schemes are key to many community development projects and underpin the major regeneration programmes. Research and experience show that, provided a community enterprise structure forms part of a community development process, there can be a range of practical outcomes. Community enterprise, as a result of development and training functions undertaken by community businesses and co-operatives, can also form part of the local economy. Crucial to all community enterprises is the achievement of a balance between community benefit and commercial trading (Twelvetrees, 1999).

Policy influence

While community development mainly takes place within neighbourhoods and communities of interest, it constantly looks to regional, national and European structures to change policies in ways which will help deprived areas. We have seen how, in the history of community development, there has been a continuing concern to link local issues to the policy agenda, and this continues today.

Equally, in terms of influencing and changing policies, community development is able to facilitate dialogue and joint initiatives between local communities and policymakers. This too is crucial, indeed it is likely to be one of the severest tests of the government's social inclusion strategy. How can communities work on a genuine partnership basis with central and local government structures – what are the essential ingredients? We return to this question in the concluding chapter.

The above examples of how community development can form part of a social inclusion strategy are rooted in wide-ranging experience of projects and initiatives in both urban and rural communities. They stand, in that sense, as instances of applied theory that contrast with the 'grander' theories of Jacobs and others, and with the practice-theory of how community workers engage with the socially excluded. All three are important. Together they demonstrate the potential for linking community development and social exclusion.

Outcomes

Increasingly, community development has come under pressure to provide evidence of how it can help to achieve improvements in living conditions and in people's lives. It is no longer possible for organisations to have open-ended community development programmes. They must be specific, targeted and costed. Evaluating community development has always been problematic because, by definition, it is to be expected that groups' objectives will change in response to new circumstances.

The model developed by the Scottish Community Development Centre – *Achieving Better Community Development* (ABCD) – is significant because it is designed to be an integral part of community development: 'if community development is to justify its role in promoting citizenship, social inclusion and learning through empowering people, it is crucial that it can identify and provide evidence about how empowerment has taken place, and how it has contributed to wider outcomes' (Barr and Hashagen, op. cit., p11).

The approach of ABCD is to define evaluation as a learning tool, 'to understand change by capturing and reflecting on as much of the process as possible, and to focus on the outcomes, not just the outputs' (ibid., p12). Ensuring a balance between quantitative and qualitative methods in evaluating community development is crucial; if the former is too dominant, the central purpose of community development will be put in jeopardy. Also, educational and attitudinal changes must be evaluated as well as more specific results – both are outcomes. Equally important is the emphasis given by ABCD to the need for a case by case approach to evaluation – use a clear framework but encourage the various stakeholders to adapt it to the particular context or locality.

As we indicated at the end of the previous chapter, we think there are still difficulties relating to information collection, including who should do the data collection, which criteria are used and who is included. Yet the importance of undertaking this kind of work is clear. If we – government and society – are serious about tackling social exclusion through community participation then we need to find out if those who are excluded are being touched by community involvement programmes and to develop ways of measuring their effectiveness. The use of longitudinal studies must be an important element in this work.

Lessons for policymakers

In order to make social inclusion programmes more effective, policy-makers need to take on board the lessons of community development:

* The challenge facing a neighbourhood-based social inclusion strategy is twofold. First, there is the reality of the complexity of communities and, especially in disadvantaged communities, the differences that exist within them. Secondly, in many deprived areas there is the feeling by local people that, over the years, their views have been ignored or sidelined by policymakers. There is a danger, paradoxically, that a social inclusion programme may actually reinforce the labelling of poor communities and people in poverty as being dependent and lacking in resourcefulness. We can see the latter point most graphically in studies of rural deprivation – the unwillingness of people who, in statistical terms are poor, yet who do not wish to be referred to as such: they may be poor in terms of income but this should not be equated, necessarily, with having a poor quality of life. In parts of rural Scotland, for example, one of the main conclusions of a research project was that: 'rural people's subjective assessment of their poverty or disadvantage tends to be at odds with objective definitions' (Shucksmith *et al.*, 1994). This unwillingness to be referred to as poor can be found in urban as well as rural communities.

* There is a need to have programmes and staff who can sustain community development over the long term. It is not only a question of resourcing projects for more than three years but also of ensuring that residents, community workers and managers are given the necessary support, such as opportunities for training, reflection and good supervision. It is crucial to recognise that skilled work is being undertaken. There can be no quick fixes when addressing the issue of social inclusion. Programmes that seek to encourage community participation within a neighbourhood renewal and regeneration framework need to acknowledge and act upon this.

* There must be structures in place, particularly in local authorities, that

ensure community development connects with policies and programmes being driven by the government priorities of community-based regeneration and social inclusion. It is for this reason that community development has to have a strong position within corporate decision-making. It cannot be on the margins of local authority policies or treated simply as a 'bolt-on' to mainstream programmes. There is a strong case for both having a corporate community development team and mainstreaming community development work in key service areas.

* There needs to be properly resourced evaluation of neighbourhood-based social inclusion programmes that meets the criteria outlined in the previous section.

These are the key lessons that policymakers can learn from the experiences of community development and social exclusion. There may at times be a tension between the need for a strategic, co-ordinated approach to community development – both within local authorities and between local, regional and national agencies – and the need to provide support for communities. A balancing act is required: both are needed. The natural tendency of policymakers is to put their weight behind strategic community development rather than the need to support communities – because of their experience of policy formulation and strategic planning. Research evidence demonstrates clearly that communities tend always to be the weakest members of local partnerships (Geddes, 1997) and if we add to this the anger and scepticism that we have suggested is prevalent in many poor communities, then there will be a high risk of losing the community's involvement in social inclusion programmes (see Martin and Boaz, 2000).

Opportunities for community development

The government's policy commitment to tackling social exclusion through neighbourhood renewal, combined with its determination to see local government changed in the direction of more open, participatory structures, means that the context in which community development is now operating is unique. This means, on the one hand, that community development has to be clear about its principles and methods. On the other hand, it means that the possibilities for community development to influence policies and programmes are probably unparalleled.

If community development is to seize the opportunities, it will need to adjust to the political and social context favoured by the government. It will also have to strengthen its own support structures. Both aims need to be realised at different levels:

- *Locally*, it is essential that the community development worker's role achieves greater recognition. National community development and regeneration organisations have a responsibility to put the arguments for this.

- *Regionally*, the government offices for the regions and regional development agencies in England must be encouraged to invest long-term in community development. Equally, the community development profession must ensure that development of regional resource centres that promote and support training and education for community development are supported and extended.

- *Nationally*, the work on capacity building and community involvement carried out with the Social Exclusion Unit's Policy Action Teams and the DETR will need to be continued and there needs to be similar work with the Scottish Executive, Welsh Assembly and Northern Ireland Office. It will be particularly important to ensure that there is a strong community development input to the neighbourhood renewal programme and to build on the opportunities given by the Community Empowerment Fund, designed to help communities develop their capacity to influence policy.

Underlying all of this there will need to be a commitment to taking forward community development practice in the context of social inclusion. It is an assessment of this that we turn to next.

4   The potential of practice

'Social inclusion is now the central issue for local government, and community development is key to it.

Assistant Chief Executive, a northern Metropolitan Council

Expectations of what community development can achieve in the context of social exclusion are rising rapidly. There must, therefore, be the question of whether it can deliver. This chapter tackles the question by looking at:

- Recent experiences of practice.
- Whether new forms of practice need to be developed.
- Ways of linking local grassroots action with local, regional and national policies.

A tale of contrasts

Working in a disadvantaged neighbourhood with people who, even within such an area, are excluded and marginalised is immensely challenging to community development organisations and practitioners. Why is this? There are several obvious points:

- Poor people will often have little self-confidence in public settings. Their self-image may be at a low level.
- Becoming involved in community action and activities may not be a priority for poor people because of their need to concentrate on survival – adequate food, shelter, health.
- People with caring responsibilities may not have the time, or may be too exhausted, to be able to become involved.
- Social security regulations may act as a deterrent to community participation.
- Poor people can find it hard to become involved in community groups because of how they are perceived by existing members, who may convey a message that oppressed people are not welcome. We are in difficult territory here, because of:

  - the historical legacy of the 'deserving' and 'undeserving' poor
  - the tendency of people who are themselves disadvantaged to be critical of those who are more oppressed than, or different from, themselves

- the likelihood that the most socially excluded members of an area will not be part of the same informal networks as others
- above all, the uncertainty, fear and suspicion which can often characterise deprived neighbourhoods:

> *The relationships and dynamics in poor communities are often tense and even dangerous, making it more difficult to come together, with security concerns often leading people to stay isolated in their homes.*
>
> (Oxfam, 1999, p7)

Community workers and other practitioners who seek to address any of these issues must think through carefully how they can act positively. Taking the issues seriously tests the real meaning of participation in local settings: in any deprived area, even the most disadvantaged, there will always be people with energy, skills and experience. To work only with such people is, arguably, not that difficult. Far more challenging is to find ways of reaching those who are most marginalised. It is here that the practitioner's skills, determination and patience, along with support from colleagues and managers, will be paramount. We know that placing an inexperienced worker on his or her own in a disadvantaged neighbourhood is likely to be a recipe for failure: there will not be the support essential for such work and, sooner or later, the worker will experience 'burn-out' and disillusionment.

If the above points are taken seriously, can we say that community development is working with the most disadvantaged groups in the poorest areas? Inevitably the picture is an uneven one. The critique of community work by Jacobs (1994) referred to in the previous chapter has some validity. He suggests that community workers are often perceived by poor people as being little different from other workers employed by statutory and voluntary organisations to work in disadvantaged communities. At another level, however, the criticism is misplaced. Community workers may not be able to bring complete solutions to the problem of social exclusion, but there can be no doubt that there is extensive experience of effective practice. The following brief case studies are designed to illustrate two aspects of practice:

- Working with a 'joined-up' solution strategy.
- Instances where the socially excluded have succeeded in getting outside bodies to intervene effectively.

Working with 'joined-up' solutions

Cutteslowe Estate, Oxford

Cutteslowe Community Network is an example of a generic community development project that includes in its activities the issue of addressing social exclusion. Readers may recall Cutteslowe as the estate which, many years ago, was literally divided from its neighbouring owner-occupiers by a wall: 'The divisions first bounded by the wall have not disappeared and changes in household tenure have not really been significant enough to alter this' (Trebilcock and Rucker, 1998, p14).

The project has tackled the deprivation of the estate by initiating and supporting a wide range of community activities and by seeking to connect its neighbourhood-based work with the agencies' policies and services. It has also made use of poverty maps prepared by Oxford University. Having set out its aims in a mission statement, it was able to look back and evaluate the extent to which it had met its objectives, especially as a focal point for the regeneration of Cutteslowe:

*   Building bridges between agencies and facilitating the emergence of a joint strategy for Cutteslowe.
*   Undertaking a community audit and research into the needs of the community on Cutteslowe and Templar Road Estates.
*   Drawing those needs to the attention of a wider audience.
*   Lobbying for support and funding.
*   Recruiting two community workers.
*   Amassing further evidence to illustrate the nature and extent of needs on Cuttleslowe.
*   Making use of this evidence to ensure that Cuttleslowe is not forgotten by decision-makers.
*   Utilising evidence of needs to design and implement intervention and support for specific groups in the community such as Sunnymeade Court residents, young people at risk and parents.
*   Creating opportunities for participation in groups, social events, activities and community initiatives – ranging from being a beneficiary of a service to helping lead an activity.

The above achievements, which are extracted from a longer list, give a flavour of the ways in which the Network has used community development principles and methods to address the issue of social exclusion. In particular, they illustrate the capacity of community development to work strategically for 'joined-up' solutions at two levels:

- Joined-up at the local level, so that activities and people relate to each other across issues and across neighbourhoods.
- Connecting local action and policymaking so that neighbourhood work operates in tandem with policy work within the agencies – mainly the local authority – which provide services for residents.

Oxfordshire County Council's strategy for tackling poverty is to maximise the opportunities available to people currently living in or vulnerable to poverty, in order to enable them to participate fully in society, both individually and as communities. 'This is exactly what Network is striving for on Cuttleslowe, particularly where young people and families with young children are concerned' (ibid., p51).

Getting outside bodies to intervene

The Poverty Alliance's mobile resource team

The Poverty Alliance is a network of voluntary organisations and community groups working across Scotland. Its mobile resource team (MRT) sought, through short-term interventions, to 'leave a legacy of increased capacity with groups, enabling them to become more influential in tackling poverty in their own communities'. The following is one of several case studies that demonstrate the range of methodologies employed by the team. In this example, the group was concerned to influence the decision-making process of the local authority with the purpose of increasing the effectiveness of services in the area.

Dumbarton and Clydebank Lone Parents

Key feature

To facilitate focus groups on the council's services to lone parents.

Background

The MRT facilitated the piloting of focus groups in Dumbarton and Clydebank to comment on the local authority's anti-poverty strategy and how it affected their community of interest. The work was undertaken in collaboration with West Dunbartonshire Council as part of its review of the first year of its strategy, the aim being to take on board users' views in order to target the resources required to meet the needs of lone parents in the next phase of the anti-poverty strategy more appropriately.

Method/process
The MRT developed a series of exercises with the lone parents to maximise participation and ensure that their views were represented. The participants commented on the delivery of the council's services to lone parents and were able to provide information to enable its departments to incorporate improvements to their service delivery.

Comment
The focus groups have led to the involvement of representatives in influencing the agenda of the council's Community Initiatives Committee – a sub-group that reports to the full council meetings on the progress of the council's cross-departmental anti-poverty strategy and voluntary sector engagement.

The council's evaluation of the pilot has led to a proposal to extend this type of consultation in the assessment of needs related to youth provision, disabled people and older people.

The two case studies demonstrate the potential for community development to contribute, often in very practical ways, to combating social exclusion. Effectiveness depends on good planning, and on agencies which fund and employ community development staff being prepared to ensure that projects are properly resourced – through teamwork, managerial support, training opportunities, monitoring and evaluation. Above all, however, it depends on there being a commitment to seeking genuine community involvement, not involvement that only engages with existing organisations, networks and leaders. This means that it is essential to give adequate time to enable the community development process to take place.

Where the two examples fall short is in being able to point to activities that contributed to reduced social exclusion. Their emphasis is on methods for carrying out the activities rather than on outcomes. This search for evidence is, as we indicated in the previous chapter, still needing to be undertaken – the ABCD evaluation model, now being used throughout the UK, provides a framework. An example of the outcomes to be looked for in community development and social inclusion programmes can be seen in the demonstration programmes run in Northern Ireland. The evaluation found that:

The greatest impact was seen in relation to community organisation. Significant progress was made in relation to personal empowerment. Performance in respect of positive action and power, relationships and participation has been positive but occurred at a slower pace.

Work in areas of weak infrastructure is possible, provided that a generic community development approach is taken and that sufficient time is given to allow progress where there is no history or understanding of the value or concept of community development. Fast-tracking this process in an effort to show quick results can be dangerous.

(Northern Ireland Voluntary Trust, 1999b, pp6-7)

Engaging with social exclusion

The following summary of ways in which community development practice can engage with social exclusion derive from a range of experiences (we are indebted to Professor Gary Craig for the ideas).

Collective responses

Autonomous community groups that use collective action and mutual solidarity are the core of community development. They can be used in social inclusion work in a variety of ways:

* Campaigns to obtain improved housing conditions or safer streets.

* Self-help activities whereby local people take responsibility for organising facilities or services, for example, a community centre, transport for disabled people, running a junior youth club.

* Employment schemes, such as community businesses and enterprise trusts, controlled by local people.

Such activities help to improve local people's living conditions. They need not necessarily be confined to neighbourhood boundaries – there are many examples of collaboration between community groups within part of a town or across an entire city. Sometimes collaboration and alliances can be built vertically as well as horizontally, as when an alliance is formed between local groups, a regeneration agency, a government working party, a charity and a company.

Counter-information

Official statistics can be presented in ways that misrepresent the experiences of exclusion – 'blaming the victim' or playing down the suffering caused by poverty. Community development can counter this kind of information, chiefly by helping excluded people to emphasise their own experiences of exclusion and finding ways of communicating these. It was the authenticity of people's experiences that made the poverty 'hearings' organised in several cities by Church Action on Poverty so powerful.

Democratic representation

Community development seeks to strengthen participatory forms of democracy. People join community groups through their own volition and exercise their right as citizens to associate freely. On occasions, demands made by groups result in disagreements with local and central government bodies whose members have been elected through the formal democratic process. It is important to understand such clashes for what they are: a genuine disagreement, a conflict of views which can be debated. Democracy needs both the representative and participatory systems. Community development is an important way of strengthening the latter.

Integrated approach

The government's insistence on 'joined-up' solutions to 'joined-up' problems resonates strongly with community development's commitment to working across issues and making links between them. Again and again we see how local people tend to prefer not to separate out community problems. For example, an action-research project set up to explore the contribution of a community development approach to community care found that community leaders and service users in each of the four areas studied all wanted to tackle the issue of caring in relation to other issues, notably transport, access and community facilities – all of which, strictly speaking, fall outside the community care legislation – yet it was essential that the project addressed them (Barr et al., 2001). There is no doubt that community development's commitment to an integrated approach has much to contribute to social inclusion strategies of central and local government.

Imaginative ideas

Community development's major resource is local people. It is dependent for its effectiveness on their enthusiasm and energy. As a result it has learnt to be good at adjusting to new suggestions and needs that arise in communities. It is a source of imaginative ideas with regard to both work methods and content: for example, suggesting forms of discussion other than a public meeting, or using community festivals and community art to celebrate 'community' alongside addressing issues of poverty, unemployment and deteriorating housing conditions. A good community worker will often discuss with local leaders the question: what will make people come out of their houses and flats to engage in public issues? What can we suggest to groups and agencies to encourage this? The answer often lies in a mix, a plurality of activities and issues.

> *Community development, with its fundamental emphasis on the partic-*
> *ipation and empowerment of the poor, reminds us that there is a need*
> *constantly to recreate other ways of living and make decisions about the*
> *distribution of material, cultural and social resources.*

(Craig, 1994)

Confidence and skills

We specified in the previous chapter how, as a result of community development intervention, it is possible to achieve outcomes that directly address social exclusion, and we have argued in the first section of this chapter that community development has delivered on many of them. Integral to these achievements, and at the core of the community development process, is increasing the confidence and skills of local people who are involved – through capacity building, training and education.

Capacity building

The term 'capacity building' has become inseparable from the policy and practice of regeneration and has been incorporated into European, government and local authority funding regimes. It is used to apply to both individuals and groups and emphasis is given to its systematic approach to helping people play a major part in the regeneration of their neighbourhood. It is:

> *Development work that strengthens the ability of community organisations*
> *and groups to build their structures, systems, people and skills so that they*
> *are better able to define and achieve their objectives and engage in*
> *consultation and planning, manage community projects and take part in*
> *partnerships and community enterprises.*

(Skinner, 1997, pp1-2)

The idea of capacity building originated in the United States and was associated with business skills and economic development. Three critical points in the context of UK regeneration programmes are:

* It has a tendency to be highly functional, i.e. equipping people with knowledge, skills and techniques to fit particular tasks and jobs rather than building their confidence or their critical awareness. Not

surprisingly, there is an emphasis on targets and measurable outcomes.

- There is often an assumption that those people targeted for capacity building are empty vessels, i.e. do not themselves have experience, knowledge and skills that can be recognised and used.

- Usually it has been applied to the less powerful side of any partnership. Until recently, there have been few examples of building up the capacity of the powerful to listen to and respect the weak. However, there is now widespread recognition that all stakeholders need to develop the capacity to work with each other. Building capacity is one way of strengthening social capital.

It is because of anxieties on these points that some commentators make the case for a re-definition of capacity building:

> Capacity building needs to move away from the predominant deficit model (for example, what skills does this sector need to participate in our agenda?) to a more participative model (for example, what does this group have to contribute to our common agenda and how can they be supported in participating fully in that process?).
> (Pan London Community Regeneration Consortium, 1999, p17).

Training

An additional outcome from the Northern Ireland Demonstration Programme described earlier was the focus on enhancing the skills and knowledge of participants, from basic skills to vocational training:

> Projects have enabled individuals to embark upon a progression route from social and basic skills to more advanced accredited training that is enhancing their confidence, self-esteem and employability. In some cases this has been linked to a local employment strategy. New leaders have emerged who can play an active role in on-going community development and represent the community in other fora.
> (Northern Ireland Voluntary Trust, op. cit., p6)

The objective of providing progression routes for members of community groups who wish to build upon their experiences of community development has gained increased recognition in recent years. The National/ Scottish Vocational Qualification in Community Work is available, at different levels, at centres across the country. A number of regional training groups, consisting of community workers and community leaders, are supported by a UK-wide federation, and active community-based training

51

initiatives have sprung up in regeneration areas. In Huyton, for example, the partnership organisation supported a course 'to fast track 12 people with the skills, knowledge and approach needed to develop community-based social and economic initiatives within their local community' (Broad, 1998). There are also several active regional training resource centres. The Bradford-based West Yorkshire Community Work Training Company, for example, provides a range of training opportunities for local people. It is linked to the University of Leeds and this facilitates the idea of progression.

Building training into community development and regeneration programmes is an obvious way of achieving sustainability over the long term: investing in training local people, who are already motivated to be involved in their communities, so that the process of strengthening communities is continued by cadres of more knowledgeable, skilled and confident leaders. This must be one of the keys which will unlock the prison of social exclusion.

Case study: Getting to know your community

Leeds City Council agreed to fund a pilot six-month training programme targeted at unemployed people in two areas of the city which face severe social and economic problems – Chapeltown and Harehills. A development worker was employed to make contact with local community organisations, and an associate trainer was used to deliver the training and obtain accreditation for the course from the Open Learning College.

The focus of the course was on community research skills and a key part of the learning was undertaking a community audit in the area. The findings of the audit will be used to inform the work of community groups and local agencies and a toolkit, based on the model of *Getting to know your community*, has been produced (Leeds City Council, 2001).

During the course the participants became increasingly interested in how the council planned its regeneration programme. The initiative is an example of how it is possible for agencies to reach out to people who can be categorised as being socially excluded but who demonstrate the extent of their potential.

The above example also illustrates how training by itself is insufficient. It has to be linked with on-going support and, indeed, with long-term commitments to resource community development in deprived neighbourhoods. Supporting involved local people to network with people carrying out similar work in other areas has also proven to be effective.

A final key point to make about training is the need to ensure that, as discussed earlier in relation to capacity building, there is also provision for practitioners and managers who are working in deprived communities. A study of training and education in regeneration areas found a high level of consensus on the benefits of having clear and comprehensive strategies for training and education. Professionals recognised their own training needs if they were to work effectively with communities in empowering ways, a view that was endorsed from the community perspective: 'The greatest need is to educate decision-makers about the voluntary sector, communities and consultation' (Henderson and Mayo, 1998, p2).

For community representatives the types of experience most positively valued are learning opportunities specifically tailored to their requirements, especially action-based learning, reinforcing and building upon learning taking place within groups. The idea of joint training, bringing together community representatives and professionals, can also have clear benefits. However, the starting point must always be an attitudinal one – that the so-called socially excluded always have something to give: 'Poor individuals and communities often feel "written off" by the rest of society, being seen as "dependent" rather than as potential agents for change both in their communities and in society as a whole' (Oxfam, op. cit., p8).

Education

The need to go beyond the idea of training to broader-based education objectives has always been a key value in community development, particularly as a way of posing questions about underlying causes of social exclusion and exploring alternative approaches to working with people. This perspective reflects the influence of Paulo Freire on adult education and community development, especially his argument that critical reflection on action taken, far from being a luxury, is of the essence to meaningful action – 'otherwise action is pure activism' (Freire, 1972, p41).

Community development's educational goals, which on the face of it sit uneasily with the present-day emphasis on measurable outcomes and outputs, mean that considerable care has to be taken when evaluating the achievements of community development in excluded communities. It is crucial for this dimension of community development to be given equal weighting to more easily visible and measurable outcomes. Recognising the need to focus on outcomes and quality of practice and change, not just outputs and quantity, is a key message of the ABCD approach to evaluation discussed earlier. Concerns that monitoring and evaluation systems in some regeneration programmes concentrate too much on specific outputs, with little attention to processes, are evident from the research undertaken in four areas as part of the Joseph Rowntree Foundation's area regeneration programme:

> *Through the research process ... many participants commented on the value of reflecting on their experiences and exchanging views. Participative monitoring and evaluation systems would enable these lessons to be shared and fed back more systematically, both locally and beyond. There was some evidence that, as a result of these learning gains, community organisations were building alliances more effectively*
>
> (Anastacio et. al., 2000, p32)

The fundamental importance of education in the community development context appears to be receiving growing attention. Part of the interest reflects the search for models of good practice in this field.

CICERO

CICERO (Community Initiatives in Citizenship Education Regionally Organised), a one-year learning project designed to develop the confidence and skills of people facing social exclusion, is addressing this concern. It operates within a European context. To join the programme individuals must:

* Be unemployed or in low-waged, part-time work.
* Have no higher or further educational qualifications.
* Be active in their local community.

Learning is at local level, where tutors run small, informal groups. CICERO has been effective in reaching existing and potential community leaders in deprived communities. There are other similar initiatives.

The growing interest in education demonstrates the connections between capacity building, training and education. But it is also a response to the government's policy of increasing the skills of people in areas of high unemployment and deprivation and matching these – it hopes – with new jobs. At the heart of regeneration programmes is an emphasis on the transmission of skills, delivered through neighbourhood learning centres and other forms of outreach, within the conceptual framework of lifelong learning. The Learning and Skills Councils will be a crucial source of support and resources for these programmes.

It is important to note an ambiguity in this context. On the one hand, learning is spoken about as a way of helping people to develop as individuals. This approach has a long tradition in adult education and community development. The assumption has been, however, that individuals will follow progression routes in order to contribute to the process of strengthening their communities. On the other hand, the emphasis on skills and knowledge development appears to be geared towards getting people back into the labour market, or entering it for the first time, and if this means them having to leave their communities then so be it. Connecting people to jobs may mean disconnecting them from communities.

It is this ambiguity which is fudging the issue of community leadership. For community development such leadership is about local people taking responsibilities and, when they serve on partnership boards and other organisations, having some form of accountability to a constituency in the community. Some community leaders may want to move into new jobs that build upon their leadership qualities. However, in the sense that the term leadership is used in community development, it is important that the idea of accountability is retained. This challenges notions that either imply an inevitability that leaders will move on from their communities to perform functions elsewhere – in enterprise companies, local authorities or partnership boards – or that distort this meaning of leadership into individualistic interpretations of the concept. The latter is demonstrated most clearly in the concept of the 'social entrepreneur' which, while located in a community setting, has a business or enterprise connotation.

Building the confidence and skills of local people should be the basis of good community development practice in poor neighbourhoods. It needs to have a higher profile – demonstrating the powerful outcomes that can be achieved and reminding policymakers of the Prime Minister's commitment to citizenship through learning made when he announced the setting up of the SEU. Community development practice should also maintain its commitment to supporting as a priority those groups in society which are most excluded and discriminated against, notably women, members of minority ethnic groups and people with disabilities.

The government's commitment to ensuring that there will be a distinct skills and knowledge strand throughout the Neighbourhood Renewal

Strategy provides the potential for strengthening this theme. Clearly there will be scope for making use of documented community development knowledge and skills alongside other disciplines and experiences.

Going beyond the local

The distinctiveness of community development's contribution to combating social exclusion lies in its commitment to working at grassroots level. When practised effectively, it is able to win the trust and involvement of local people, even those who are classified as being socially excluded or who may be disillusioned with participation and partnerships. Any dilution of this approach would leave community development seriously weakened, particularly in the context of social exclusion.

At the same time, community development has learnt that, if it is to facilitate change in communities, it has to go beyond the local. Employing community workers only to work on a neighbourhood basis has been shown to be insufficient. The key components of a community development strategy which take it outside a wholly neighbourhood framework are outlined below.

Policy work

In addition to having managers who can provide proper support for community workers, community development needs to have staff inside organisations who can 'champion' its principles, methods and outcomes. Local authorities are the key organisations but a similar organisational commitment to community development is required by voluntary organisations, regeneration agencies and health authorities/departments.

The case for placing community development near the centre of local authorities' decision-making processes is now very strong. This is because of the extent to which government policies on social inclusion, regeneration, Best Value and Community Strategies require local authorities to change how they relate to communities: decentralisation of services, elected members focusing their energies on area assemblies and forums, an insistence on local authorities consulting communities on their plans. Arguably, they cannot begin to shift into this new world unless they have a community development strategy.

Community development policy work in large organisations is high risk in terms of retaining the cutting edge of community development. This is because of the ease with which it can be absorbed into organisational procedures and made, as it were, to work on behalf of the organisation rather than communities – a form of cooption to which community workers and others should be very alert because of past experiences of local activists being drawn into a similar process. The risk, however, is worth taking because the potential outcomes of the policy dimension for excluded people are considerable. It means that community development can influence how resources are allocated, the ways in which services are delivered and decision-making processes by elected members to an extent which, if it stayed only within a neighbourhood framework, it could never do.

Regional work

We have noted already how community work training is available within regions. With government offices for the regions and regional development agencies playing key roles in supporting and resourcing regeneration programmes, the case for community development to operate at a regional level in England is clear. Community groups are involved in regional forums for voluntary and community organisations and other networks. Their participation regionally is especially important in those areas which are eligible for Objective 1, 2 and 3 funding from the European Union because it is in these areas that the need to make the connections between community development and social exclusion is most evident.

Four nations work

The regional agenda in England, devolution in Scotland and Wales and the special circumstances of Northern Ireland mean that community development is having to re-think how it organises itself within the UK, engaging with the new structures in each of the four nations while at the same time retaining a UK-wide perspective. This is particularly important for projects and workers wishing to share good practice on community development and social exclusion. It is essential that learning and exchange continues across the four nations.

National and international work

Finding the resources to strengthen community development's commitment to combating social exclusion at national and international levels is also vital in order to:

* Disseminate evidence of how community development supports social inclusion.
* Make links between organisations whose priority is anti-poverty work and organisations with a community development remit.
* Contribute experiences of local people to national policy debates such as those initiated by the work of the SEU.

There are a number of anti-poverty and community development organisations and networks with UK-wide remits. As well as keeping the issue of social inclusion and community development on their agendas there is also a need to sustain and develop the links between them. We made reference earlier to Oxfam's perspective on social exclusion, much of which is drawn from its long experience in southern countries. In the European context, there are links between the European Anti-Poverty Network and community development networks such as the Combined European Bureau for Social Development.

Voices of the socially excluded

Without wishing to detract from the SEU's emphasis on involving local people, we would add two caveats:

• There is danger of placing unfair and unrealistic expectations on those living in deprived neighbourhoods. The SEU tends to exaggerate the potential for involving local people, because it fails to grasp the complexity and variation between neighbourhoods. Both sociological theory and community development practice show that disadvantaged neighbourhoods vary greatly between those which, at one extreme, are stable, homogeneous and have strong common bonds, and those which, at the other extreme, are varied in composition, lack a sense of cohesion and have high levels of mobility. Attempts to involve people are more likely to be successful in the more stable neighbourhoods than in those which are more complex and fluid.

• There is a risk that some might see the emphasis upon capacity building – desirable in itself – as a way of dumping wider societal problems on the excluded. Hovering around some of the notions of self-help and social entrepreneurial activities are echoes of Etzioni's brand of communitarianism with its emphasis upon rights and responsibilities of ordinary people while neglecting the responsibilities of the rich and the powerful. This approach relates to Levitas's analysis to which we refer in chapter 2: it reflects her moral discourse and has nothing in common with the redistribution discourse. An analysis of the statements of government ministers shows that they are placed mainly between the integrationist discourse and the moral discourse and only occasionally adopt the redistribution mode.

Critical reflection

In this chapter we have sought to demonstrate ways in which community development practice can contribute to social inclusion, summarised how participatory forms of capacity building, training and education are fundamental to community development and argued that community development has to operate outside as well as within neighbourhoods. At the same time, we have indicated areas where, because of the changing policy context, community development needs to be more involved.

Our final point relates both to the neighbourhood and to activities beyond it, and draws upon both current and past experiences. A major weakness in policymaking, and one which is illustrated very obviously today, is the tendency to become trapped in a project culture, one initiative following another. Funding is made available for specified periods to address particular topics, and organisations are invited to apply for funding to run projects. It is a pragmatic approach in which all 'stakeholders' – government departments, local authorities, voluntary organisations, community groups, companies – are caught up. The problem is that such a system does not encourage critical reflection or learning. Yet there is no shortage of evaluative material from neighbourhoods concerning the impact of policies on the lives of local people.

Community development is in a position to promote serious analysis of social inclusion programmes, notably to pose difficult questions about:

- Power differences within communities and how those people who are most marginalised experience both external interventions by organisations and the work of active citizens who live in the same communities.
- Experiences of participation and consultation: who gets involved and on what basis. CDF's research department has begun to develop longitudinal methods for evaluating community development projects so that this vital question can be addressed.

We discuss in the final chapter how such a questioning role for community development can form part of a more concerted joining together of community development and social inclusion.

5 Conclusions

Since the late 1960s governments have launched a succession of schemes to deal with deprivation and the need for regeneration. These have usually been in response to a crisis or to growing public concern about poverty in an affluent society. The 1997 government announced its intention of 'tackling social exclusion' within months of being elected and it immediately began to put in place mechanisms by which this ambitious undertaking could be achieved. The 2001 government is committed to continuing the undertaking.

Bold strategy

The 1997 government launched a more comprehensive and larger scale approach to dealing with neighbourhood deprivation than had ever previously been adopted. 'Bringing Britain Together' and 'tackling social exclusion' were the sloganised expressions of the strategy's aims. The importance attached to the initiative was demonstrated by the Prime Minister's personal involvement and by locating the SEU within the Cabinet Office.

In chapter 2 we showed that social exclusion is both complex and controversial. Its precise meaning is not immediately apparent, and different ideological slants can be given to its use. It does, however, have an advantage over more static concepts. It is multi-dimensional, dynamic in nature and is a process that can reflect varying degrees of exclusion. By drawing attention to the factors contributing to the experience – unemployment, lack of skills, bad health, housing etc – it enables appropriate linked responses to be formulated. Hence the attention given to 'joined-up solutions' to 'joined-up problems'.

The consistent emphasis on the involvement of local people and the importance of taking the views of those living in deprived neighbourhoods seriously are commendable features of the government's strategy. It is this aspect that creates favourable conditions for community development to make a contribution. Also, the government recognises the inadequacy of short-term funding, and accepts that initiatives need to be sustained over a longer period than in the past. The illustration used earlier of Hillfields in Coventry suggests that even ten years may not be long enough to make lasting changes.

It is also to the SEU's credit that it has involved a wide spectrum of people with expertise in its PATs. What does remain unclear, however, is the extent to which these teams have drawn on the direct experiences of the excluded. It is not easy to draw people into formal structures, but a 'focus group' approach such as that adopted by the Poverty Alliance's mobile resource team referred to in chapter 4 would have been a way of bridging the gap. The same method could have been used to engage those living in deprived areas in the consultation process on the Neighbourhood Renewal Strategy.

Next stage

The SEU's 2001 report outlines the future strategy. It reiterates the government's aims and offers a tantalising vision of a society in which no one will need to suffer exclusion because of where she or he lives. The crucial question is: will the new strategy enable the declared aim of ending neighbourhood deprivation and 'Bringing Britain Together' to be realised? Will a greater sense of social cohesion be generated as a result of the imagination, effort and resources which are being devoted to the effort? Community development workers and others involved at a neighbourhood level will have a crucial contribution to make but, as we have already commented, their work can only take us so far.

Obviously the SEU feels that it has produced in the 2001 report a strategy that can deliver the kind of society envisioned. A great range of policies, statistics, targets and ideas are presented under familiar headings. The analysis of causes is similar to that presented in earlier reports. The section on social and economic changes rehearses six factors, only one of which is really about economic change. A second refers to rising skill demands. There is still a reluctance to refer to the vast inequalities in our society compared with most other EU countries.

A Neighbourhood Renewal Fund will have £900 million to dispense over three year periods to the 88 local authority districts identified as the most deprived. This represents an increase of £100 million over the sum quoted in the SEU's report. During 2001 £200 million is available; this will be increased to £300 million in each of the two subsequent years. Forty-five million pounds will be spent on at least two rounds of Neighbourhood Management pathfinders over the next three years. Local authorities are also now expected to prioritise targeted areas in their mainstream allocation of money.

Approximately £400,000 of other money will be given to 'communities in the most deprived districts in each of the three years to participate in Local Strategic Partnerships (LSPs) through the Community Empowerment Fund...'. Community Chests will fund local small grant schemes so that communities can run their own projects.

It appears, therefore, that the climate is such that community development will probably be more secure than it has ever been. After a period when it has struggled for funds and the number of workers has declined, it should now have greater recognition and be able to use its experience to the benefit of the most deprived sections of the population in the 88 designated areas. It will also be easier for potential local leaders to obtain training and for those engaged in locally inspired projects to develop their skills. This will be part of what is termed 'capacity building'.

The organisational structure being established is probably impressive in managerial terms, but it is likely to be seen as a bureaucratic jungle by the local activist. It does raise the question as to whether the 'architects' of the structure have fully taken into account the 'builders' on the ground. Workers and activists will have to familiarise themselves with a new set of acronyms and the role of the new bodies.

More than 90 examples of what is described as 'good practice' at a local level are listed in the SEU's 2001 report. They make fascinating and interesting reading, but it is too early to judge their longevity or long-term effectiveness, or to see how they fit into 'joined-up' solutions to multi-faceted problems. At their best, they will make a tiny difference unless they are matched by many other simultaneous efforts to bring about change. One illustration is of an effective super-caretaker scheme in Hartlepool, which has reduced crime by 35 per cent over three years on one estate. However, at the same time unemployment continues to be very high. The former chairperson of the Hartlepool Enterprise Agency complained in a letter to the Prime Minister about the 'North-South Divide. The unacceptable 10.2 per cent unemployment in Hartlepool' (*New Statesman*, 25 September 2000, pp43-4).

To sum up: there is much in the report to encourage those concerned with the plight of deprived areas. Certainly there is a very positive recognition of the need to take the views of local people seriously and to make provision for people to participate in joint enterprises and to run their own projects. Community development agencies and workers will welcome this with the proviso that it is for local people to make their own choices.

Civil society

Community, participation and self-help, which figure prominently in the SEU's work, all link to civil society. A government – through decentralisation, by stressing the role of local people and by providing practical support to community groups – can help to create the conditions for a strong civil society. However, it cannot and should not try to shape it.

Civil society is based upon common bonds and the formation of self-determining groups and organisations. These tend to emerge over a decade or more in a climate which is favourable to such developments. Russia and Eastern Europe have a weak civil society: a legacy of centralised control throughout the Communist period. In the UK, the 18 years of Conservative government engendered an individualistic, competitive ethos which was not conducive to a strong civil society. It was only towards the end of this period that senior politicians such as Douglas Hurd rediscovered the need for 'active citizens', voluntary activity and communities. The end product of both totalitarian and highly competitive societies is more likely to be individualism and consumerism than community and social responsibility. It will take years for civil society to strengthen, and this is likely to be particularly the case in some deprived neighbourhoods. But a strong civil society in a favourable climate can help to generate greater cohesion and feeling of inclusion.

Yet, while the messages are mixed, we do have a government which is creating some of the conditions for a dynamic civil society. Unfortunately, at the same time there are signs of social engineering, mainly in areas with cumulative problems. Why, for example, is self-help more important in poor than in affluent areas? And why does the absence of 'strong communities' and the fact that people do not 'know each other' in poor areas produce a sense of 'stranger danger', whereas in more prosperous areas the absence of such communities, and the prevalence of privacy and anonymity, do not present problems?

Bringing Britain Together (1998) sparked this tendency when it asked the self-help Policy Action Team to prepare a plan to 'raise the numbers involved in volunteering and community activity in poor neighbourhoods'. Does this mean that 'richer' areas already have the appropriate numbers volunteering and engaging in 'community activity'? These are virtuous things for people to do providing they arise naturally. Though the PAT 9 report says that 'community self-help is not something that can be imposed', the impression conveyed is that it is an essential element in neighbourhood renewal. Certainly it can help, but many areas seem to manage very well without it.

Community development believes in the need for a vigorous civil society. It believes that it is an essential feature of a healthy and cohesive society and all sections of the population need to participate in it. Community development has many years of experience in stimulating local activity and involvement, supporting emerging groups, engaging in capacity building and cultivating leadership talent in areas where there is a shortage of the necessary skills.

Community development and 'joined-up' solutions

In chapter 3 we distinguished between the different ways in which the term 'participation' can be used. We have also defined what is meant by community involvement and community development in the context of social exclusion. The problem with the term 'self-help' is that it does not convey the potential of community-based social inclusion work.

Community development has an important contribution to make in helping to generate a sense of social inclusion. It is also important that it delivers 'value for money' irrespective of the overall context within which it is operating, and we have described some of the achievements of community development in chapters 3 and 4. However, both geographically targeted initiatives and the local activities of community workers are likely to be more productive when residents of deprived neighbourhoods can see evidence that those exercising power are creating a fairer and more equal society.

Our argument is that, in order to realise the vision of a society in which, within ten to twenty years, no one is seriously disadvantaged by where they live, there will need to be more than a creditable renewal strategy for deprived neighbourhoods. Intervention on the ground needs to be sustained and supported by wider changes. In the past the impact of programmes and initiatives has been limited because they have not been part of wider policies to reduce inequality. Both policymakers and community development professionals need to remember that many people live outside designated action areas and zones. Neighbourhood-based programmes can only be one component of a broader social inclusion strategy.

When there is a link between macro-policy, geographically based initiatives and working with people directly, we will be near to delivering a 'joined-up' solution to the problems of deprived neighbourhoods. Only then will it be likely that the experiences of areas like Hillfields will not be repeated.

Finally, we need to make four key points relating to community development.

Learning lessons

There is a large body of knowledge, accumulated over the past 40 years, which can provide essential guidance on how to intervene in deprived neighbourhoods and on how to work with local people. It also gives crucial insights into the opportunities and constraints for participation in deprived areas, especially in relation to the issues of gender and race. Common sense suggests that policymakers responsible for social inclusion and regeneration programmes need to ensure that the lessons from past experience are understood and applied – otherwise it is predictable that projects will make similar mistakes to those made in earlier initiatives.

It is equally crucial that those individuals and organisations involved in community development take forward their learning from the programmes and initiatives designed to combat social exclusion. The phrase 'modernising community development' is beginning to appear. Its implications need to be addressed at the level of practice (neighbourhood work skills, use of new technology), policy (e.g. Local Strategic Partnerships), training and theory. There is a danger that the capacity of community development in these areas will lag behind expectations held of it.

Strategy and resources

The government placed a duty on local authorities in England and Wales in the Local Government Act 2000 to prepare community strategies for promoting the economic, environmental and social well-being of their areas. This, together with the fact that local authorities have also been given a major role in delivering and co-ordinating neighbourhood initiatives to combat social exclusion, means that they will need to take a more strategic approach to community development. This will require it to be resourced properly. There is some catching-up to do here. While the grant-making and appraisal sections of the local authorities have expanded to deal with government and European funding regimes, there is no evidence that the number of frontline practitioners has so far increased: 'Community development work is not being prioritised as a specific activity in many programmes ... There is only limited evidence that regeneration programmes have successfully moved from enabling to empowering communities during their lifetime' (Duncan and Thomas, 2000, p24).

The weakness of community development, in strategic and resource terms, within local authorities and regeneration programmes may prove to be a serious constraint on fulfilling the ambitions of social inclusion and regeneration. However, there is now the prospect that this will change. The survey of community workers being undertaken by the Standing Conference for Community Development in 2001-2002 will provide evidence of the strengths and weaknesses of the profession and the kinds of resources that community development needs if it is to deliver.

Working with uncertainties

Community development operates in unpredictable and dynamic situations. As we pointed out earlier, neighbourhoods vary tremendously in their potential for collaborative action and part of the initial process is about assessing the area, asking questions, testing responses, determining who are the most excluded and establishing whether people are prepared to accept support from a worker. Even if the circumstances are conducive to community development, the effectiveness of any intervention will depend upon local people deciding the needs and priorities with which they are prepared to become involved. Many agencies find it very difficult to keep faith with this principle, usually because they are under pressure to deliver specific outcomes at set times. As a result, it is very easy for community-agency partnerships to fragment.

There is recognition in SEU's third report of the complexity of neighbourhoods and also of the difficulties associated in involving local people. The essential point that the government, local authorities and health and regeneration agencies need to acknowledge is the right of local groups to make their own decisions. These are influenced both by the diversity of neighbourhoods and by the competing needs and issues which face local people – especially those who are poor and excluded. A community group may decide to focus on an issue which, to external agencies, may not appear to be a priority. The point is that it is the group's right to make such a decision, and agencies need to respect that and find ways of returning to the issues on their agenda.

Somehow, therefore, social exclusion and regeneration programmes have to become better at working with uncertainties in communities, being prepared to take risks as well as to change direction at different stages of their involvement. Communities – how they work, memories of earlier projects, overt and covert tensions, who is trusted and who is not – do not fit easily with notions of carefully controlled, externally-driven programmes.

Feedback and change

The dynamic and complex nature of the community development process means that considerable attention has to be given to ensuring that there are rigorous ways of obtaining feedback from communities and evaluating work undertaken. Employers of community workers need regular reporting systems so that decisions of senior managers and elected members are informed by accurate information from work carried out with community groups. There also need to be area-based forums at which local people can discuss with elected members and officials how social inclusion and regeneration programmes are being experienced. Finally, evaluation of community development should form an integral part of planning and resourcing programmes.

Ensuring feedback and having the capacity to change the design of programmes are central to effective local strategies. They relate to our argument at the end of the previous chapter for greater recognition of how community development can contribute critical reflection to programmes. However, the effectiveness of neighbourhood-based social inclusion programmes depends on more than this and the other points outlined above. Discussion of how to put into practice meaningful policies aimed at combating social exclusion are inseparable, as we have earlier indicated, from broader policy decisions.

Abbreviations

ABCD	Achieving Better Community Development
BASSAC	British Association of Settlements and Social Action Centres
CDF	Community Development Foundation
CDP	Community Development Projects
CICERO	Community Initiatives in Citizenship Education Regionally Organised
DETR	Department of the Environment, Transport and the Regions
DTLR	Department for Transport, Local Government and the Regions
EU	European Union
GTI	Geographically Targeted Initiatives
JRF	Joseph Rowntree Foundation
LETS	Local Exchange Trading Schemes
LNRS	Local Neighbourhood Renewal Strategy
LSP	Local Strategies Partnership
MRT	Mobile Resource Team
NIVT	Northern Ireland Voluntary Trust
NRF	Neighbourhood Resource Fund
NRU	Neighbourhood Renewal Unit
PLCRC	Pan London Community Regeneration Consortium
PAT	Policy Action Team
RDA	Regional Development Agency
SCCD	Standing Conference for Community Development
SCDC	Scottish Community Development Centre
SEU	Social Exclusion Unit
SRB	Single Regeneration Budget

References

Acheson, D. (1998) *Report of the Independent Inquiry into Inequalities in Health*, London: The Stationery Office

Alcock, P. (1997) *Understanding Poverty*, Basingstoke: Macmillan

Anastacio, J. *et al.* (2000) *Reflecting Realities*, Bristol: The Policy Press

Arnstein, S. (1969) 'A Ladder of Public Participation', *Journal of the American Institute of Planners*. See Ashton, J. 'Going Strategic Locally' in P. Ashton and A. Hobbs (eds) (2000) *Communities Developing for Health*, Liverpool: Health for All Network (UK) Ltd (p136)

Atkinson, A.B. (1998) *Social Exclusion, Poverty and Unemployment in Exclusion, Employment and Opportunity*, London: Centre for Analysis of Social Exclusion

Barr, A. and Hashagen, S. (2000) *ABCD Handbook*, London: CDF Publications

Barr, A., Stenhouse, C. and Henderson, P. (2001) *Caring Communities. A Challenge for Social Inclusion*, York: Joseph Rowntree Foundation

Brager, G. and Specht, H. (1973), *Community Organizing*, New York: Columbia University Press

Broad, C. (1998) *Huyton Partnership Community Development Training and Progression*, Liverpool: Comment, p3

Burghardt, S. (1982) *Organizing for Community Action*, Beverly Hills, Cal: Sage Publications

Byrne, D. (1999) *Social Exclusion*, Buckingham: Oxford University Press

Chanan, G., Garratt, C. and West, A. (2000) *The New Community Strategies*, London: CDF Publications

Chanan, G., Gilchrist, A. and West, A. (1999) *SRB 6: Involving the Community*, London: CDF Publications

Commission on Poverty, Participation and Power (2000) *Listen Hear. The Right to be Heard*, Bristol: Policy Press in association with UK Coalition on Poverty

Commission on Social Justice (1994) *Social Justice: Strategies for National Renewal*, London: Vintage

Coventry CDP (1975) *Coventry and Hillfields: Prosperity, and the Persistence of Inequality*, Coventry CDP/Institute of Local Government Studies

Craig, G. (1994) 'Social Exclusion and Community Development' in *Policy for Practice*, seminar papers, Glasgow: SCDC

DETR (2000a) *Indices of Deprivation 2000*, London: DETR

DETR (2000b) *Preparing Community Strategies. Government Guidance to Local Authorities*, London: DETR

Donnison, D. (1998) *Policies for a Just Society*, London: Macmillan

Duncan, P. and Thomas, S. (2000) *Neighbourhood Regeneration*, Bristol: The Policy Press

Durham County Council (1999) *Community Development – Strategy and Action Plan*, Durham: Durham County Council

Eade, D. (1997) *Capacity-Building. An Approach to People-Centred Development*, Oxford: Oxfam (UK and Ireland)

Fairclough, N. (2000) *New Labour, New Language?*, London: Routledge

Fimister, G. (2001) (ed) *End in Sight*, London: CPAG

Freire, P. (1972) *Pedagogy of the Oppressed*, Harmondsworth: Penguin

Galbraith, J. K. (1993) *The Culture of Contentment*, London: Penguin Books

Galbraith, J. K. (1996) *The Good Society: The Humane Agenda*, London: Sinclair-Venson

Gaventa, J. (1998) 'Poverty, Participation and Social Exclusion in North and South', *IDS Bulletin*, 29 (1) pp50-57

Geddes, M. (1997) *Partnership against Poverty and Exclusion?*, Bristol: The Policy Press

Geddes, M. (2000) *Strategies for Social Inclusion: Learning from Scottish Experience*, Local Authorities and Social Exclusion Network Research Paper 1, Local Government Centre, University of Warwick, London: Local Government Information Unit

Gittell, R. and Vidal, A. (1998) *Community Organizing, Thousand Oaks*, Cal: Sage Publications

Gray, J. (2000) 'Inclusion: A Radical Critique' in P. Askonas and A. Stewart (eds) *Social Inclusion: Possibilities and Tensions*, Basingstoke: Macmillan

Hashagen, S. (1998) *Strengthening Communities. Tackling Health Inequalities through Community Action*, Edinburgh: Health Education Board for Scotland

Henderson, P. (1997) *Social Inclusion and Citizenship in Europe: The Contribution of Community Development*, The Hague: Dr Gradus Hendriks Stichting/CEBSD

Henderson, P. and Mayo, M. (1998) *Training and Education in Urban Regeneration*, Bristol: The Policy Press

Henderson, P. and Salmon, H. (1998) *Signposts to Local Democracy*, London: CDF Publications

Higgins, K. (1978) *The Poverty Business*, Oxford: Blackwell and Mott Ltd

Home Office (1999) *Report of the Policy Action Team on Community Self-Help*, London: Active Community Unit, Home Office

Jacobs, S. (1994) 'Community Work in a Changing World' in S. Jacobs and K. Popple (eds) *Community Work in the 1990s*, Nottingham: Spokesman

Joseph Rowntree Foundation (1999 and 2000) *Monitoring Poverty and Social Exclusion*, York: Joseph Rowntree Foundation

Kawachi, I. *et al.* (1996) Social Capital, Income Inequality and Mortality, *American Journal of Public Health*, summer 1997

Killeen, D. (1999) 'Scotland's Distinctive Approach', *Poverty Matters*, 20, London: IDeA, pp17-19

Leeds City Council (2001) *Getting to Know Your Community Toolkit*, Leeds: Housing and Environmental Health Services, Leeds City Council

Levitas, R. (1998) *The Inclusive Society? Social Exclusion and New Labour*, London: Macmillan

Lister, R. (2000) 'Strategies for Social Inclusion: Promoting Social Cohesion or Social Justice?' in P. Askonas and A. Stewart (eds) *Social Inclusion Possibilities and Tensions*, London: Macmillan

Lister, R. (2001) 'Doing Good by Stealth: the Politics of Poverty and Inequality Under New Labour', *New Economy*, 8 (2)

Martin, S. and Boaz, S. (2000) 'Public Participation and Citizen-Centred Local Government: Letters from the Best Value and Better Government for Older People Pilot Programmes', *Public Money and Management*, 20 (2) pp47-54, Oxford: Blackwell

Micklewright, J. and Stewart. K. (2000) 'Child Well-Being and Social Cohesion: Is the UK the Oddball in Europe?', *New Economy*, 7 (1) pp14-17

Murray, C. (1990) *The Emerging British Underclass*, London: Institute of Economic Affairs

Murray, C. (1994) *The Underclass*, London: Institute of Economic Affairs

Northern Ireland Voluntary Trust (1999a) *Social Inclusion. Lessons from the Peace Programme*, Belfast: NIVT

Northern Ireland Voluntary Trust (1999b) *Building Community Infrastructure. Lessons from the Community Development Demonstration Programmes*, Belfast: NIVT

Oppenheim, C. (1998) 'An Overview of Poverty and Social Exclusion' in C. Oppenheim *An Inclusive Society*, London: IPPR

Oxfam (1999) *Report of the Policy Action Team on Self-Help*, Oxford: Oxfam GB

Pan London Community Regeneration Consortium (1999) *Capacity Building ... the Way Forward*, London: PLCRC

Pearson, S., Kirkpatrick, A. and Barnes, C. (1997) *Local Poverty, Local Responses*, Sheffield: Sheffield Hallam University and University of Lincolnshire and Humberside

Plowden, W. (2000) 'Joined-up Government', *The Guardian*, March 8

The Poverty Alliance (1999) *Resources on Tap*, Glasgow: The Poverty Alliance

Putnam, R.B. (1993) *Making Democracy Work: Civic Traditions in Modern Italy*, Princeton, NJ: Princeton University Press

Putnam, R.B. (1995) 'Bowling Alone: America's Declining Social Capital', *Journal of Democracy* 6 (1) pp65-78

Putnam, R.B. (2000) *Bowling Alone: The Collapse and Revival of American Community*, New York: Simon and Shuster

Robson, B. *et al.* (1994) *Assessing the Impact of Urban Policy*, London: HMSO

Room, G. (1993) *Anti-Poverty Action Research in Europe*, Bristol: School for Advanced Urban Studies

Root, A. (2000) *The Role of Geographically Targeted Initiatives*, Research Paper 2, Local Government Centre, University of Warwick London: LGIU

Salmon, H. (1998) 'Ending Social Exclusion: can Labour Deliver?', *Renewal*, 6 (3)

Shucksmith, M. *et al.* (1994) *Disadvantage in Rural Scotland*, summary report, Aberdeen: University of Aberdeen

Skinner, S. (1997) *Building Community Strengths*, London: CDF Publications

Sloggett, A. and Joshi, H. (1994) *Higher Mortality in Deprived Areas: Community or Personal Disadvantage?*, London: London School of Hygiene and Tropical Medicine

SEU (1998) *Bringing Britain Together: A National Strategy for Neighbourhood Renewal*, London: The Stationery Office

SEU (2000a) *National Strategy for Neighbourhood Renewal: a Framework for Consultation*, London: The Stationery Office

SEU (2000b) *Minority Ethnic Issues in Social Exclusion and Neighbourhood Renewal*, London: The Stationery Office

SEU (2001) *A New Commitment to Neighbourhood Renewal*, London: The Stationery Office

Standing Conference for Community Development (1992) *A Working Statement on Community Development*, Sheffield: SCCD

Standing Conference for Community Development (2001) *A Strategic Framework for Community Development*, Sheffield: SCCD

Therborn, G. (1985) *Why Some Peoples are More Unemployed than Others*, London: Verso

Townsend, P. (1979) *Poverty in the United Kingdom: a Survey of Household Resources and Standards of Living*, London: Penguin

Trebilcock, D. and Rucker, K. (1998) *Cutteslowe Community Report*, Oxford: Cutteslowe Community Network

Twelvetrees, A. (1999) *Community Economic Development: Rhetoric or Reality?*, London: CDF Publications

Wacquant, L.D. (1996) 'Red Belt, Black Belt: Racial Division, Class Inequality and the State in the French Urban Periphery and the American Ghetto' in E. Mingione (ed) *Urban Poverty and the Underclass*, Oxford: Blackwell

West, A. and McCormick, J. (1998) 'Three Steps and Beyond: Micro-Economies for Social Inclusion' in C. Oppenheim (ed) *An Inclusive Society: Strategies for Tackling Poverty*, London: IPPR

Wilkinson, R. G. (1996) *Unhealthy Societies: The Afflictions of Inequality*, London: Routledge

Woods, R. (2000) *Mainstream Services, Best Value and Social Inclusion*, Local Government Centre, University of Warwick, London: LGIU

Community Development Foundation Publications

The following titles are also available:

Community Development and Rural Issues - new edition

David Francis and Paul Henderson with James Derounian

Rural poverty and wide-ranging environmental concerns are some of the problems driving an increasing public debate across the UK on rural matters. This revised and updated briefing paper assesses the contribution which community development makes to rural concerns.

The authors set the rural context, identify broad trends in rural issues, and provide examples of effective community work in various settings including housing, environmental action, village services, village halls, community centres and village appraisals. They identify the main agencies, programmes and action in the UK and show why it is vital that changes in rural areas resulting from government and European programmes, devolution and regionalisation in England are informed and influenced by the people who live and work there.

£6.00, 34pp, A5, ISBN 0 901974 02 2, 2nd edition 2001

Rural Racism in the UK
Examples of community-based responses

Edited by Paul Henderson and Ranjit Kaur

This book observes racism in a rural context and offers solutions using a community development framework. The editors establish the reality and extent of racism in rural communities and use case studies to illustrate how community-based responses can help to confront the problem. Written by experienced practitioners in consultation with members of local organisations, the book contains powerful messages for local, regional and national agencies providing services and advice to rural communities.

£8.95, 77pp, ISBN 1 901974 12 X 1999

Needs Not Numbers
An exploration of minority ethnic communities in Scotland
Philomena JF de Lima

The first study to explore the experiences of minority ethnic households across four rural areas of Scotland reveals that the experiences of these groups are complex and cannot be understood using a simple urban/rural distinction. Whilst both rural and urban minority ethnic dwellers experience racial discrimination in accessing services generally, and particularly in relation to employment and language support, the rural experience is compounded by the fact that the groups are isolated and lack access to community networks and support. The absence in most rural areas of an infrastructure which tackles racism exacerbates the problem.

This study emphasises that the size, diversity and dispersed nature of minority ethnic groups in rural areas means that creative solutions will have to be found and new models of service delivery will have to be developed if the inequalities which these groups face are to be effectively tackled.
£5.00, 70pp, A5, ISBN 1 901974 24 3 2001

Building Practitioner Strengths
Reflecting on community development practice
Mandy Wilson and Pete Wilde

This handbook provides accounts from workers operating in a range of contexts and offers a framework through which practitioners can examine and reflect on their practice. Guidelines and examples illustrate the stages involved, and help develop a reflective framework.
£14.95, 120pp, ISBN 1 901974 19 7 2001

Signposts to Community Development (2nd edition)
Marilyn Taylor, Alan Barr and Alison West

Revised and updated, this briefing paper provides a snapshot of the history, methods, and values of community development in the UK. Concludes with a select bibliography and list of essential contacts in the UK and mainland Europe.
£6.95, 44pp, ISBN 1 901974 03 0 2001

Achieving Better Community Development

This set of three publications provides all the material to take an organi-sation, group of workers or trainees through the ABCD process - a method for understanding and evaluating community development.

ABCD Handbook: a framework for evaluating community development

Alan Barr and Stuart Hashagen

This core text describes the ABCD approach, discusses the components of community development in detail, and sets out the stages for planning and evaluating it.

£9.95, 92pp, ISBN 1 901974 20 0 2000

Achieving Better Community Development: trainers' resource pack

Alan Barr and Stuart Hashagen

All the materials necessary to deliver training in ABCD. Can only be used in conjunction with the ABCD Handbook.

£27.00, 110pp in ring-binder, ISBN 1 901974 22 7 2000

Working with ABCD: experience, lessons and issues from practice

Peter Taylor with Alan Barr and Stuart Hashagen

Case studies showing different applications of ABCD in Britain and Ireland, with a commentary on the lessons for policy and practice.

£14.95, 50pp, ISBN 1 901974 21 9 2000

All prices are exclusive of postage and packing
A full list of our publications is available from:
Publication Orders, Community Development Foundation
60 Highbury Grove
London N5 2AG
tel 020 7226 5375
email admin@cdf.org.uk website www.cdf.org.uk